SCIENCE AnyTime™

Workbook

HARCOURT BRACE & COMPANY

Orlando Atlanta Austin Boston San Francisco Chicago Dallas New York
Toronto London

Copyright © by Harcourt Brace & Company

All rights reserved. No part of this publication may be reproduced or transmitted in any form or by any means, electronic or mechanical, including photocopy, recording, or any information storage and retrieval system.

Permission is granted for the printing of complete pages for instructional use and not for resale by any teacher using SCIENCE ANYTIME.

HARCOURT BRACE and Quill Design is a registered trademark of Harcourt Brace & Company.

Printed in the United States of America

ISBN 0-15-306787-X

1 2 3 4 5 6 7 8 9 10   085   98 97 96 95

SCIENCE AnyTime™
Workbook

CONTENTS

UNIT A Weather Watch
- Section A • How's the Weather? **A1**
- Section B • Storm Warning **A7**
- Section C • Different Places, Different Weather **A12**

UNIT B The Inside Story
- Section A • Cells **B1**
- Section B • We're Organized **B7**
- Section C • In Sickness and in Health **B10**

UNIT C StarBase Earth
- Section A • Going Around Together **C1**
- Section B • Close to Home **C6**
- Section C • Stars Above **C11**
- Section D • Stars Near and Far **C16**

UNIT D Cooking with Science
- Section A • Properties of Matter **D1**
- Section B • Changes in Matter **D5**
- Section C • Heat **D11**

UNIT E Prairie Dog Tales
- Section A • Life on the Prairie **E1**
- Section B • Cycles and Soil **E7**
- Section C • World Biomes **E12**
- Section D • People and the Prairie **E16**

UNIT F Amusement Park
- Section A • How Does It Move? **F1**
- Section B • Pushes and Pulls **F6**
- Section C • The Forces Are with You **F11**
- Section D • Work and Machines **F16**

Name _____ Date _____

SECTION A WORKBOOK

How's the Weather?

Science Concept

A combination of factors, such as the sun's rays and the wind, interact to cause local weather conditions.

Vocabulary (pages A94–A95)

local winds	air mass	precipitation
front	prevailing winds	forecast
barometer	air pressure	water cycle

Lesson 1 Summary (pages A13–A17)

Read the summary, and then answer the questions that follow.

People have always tried to predict the weather. Before there were accurate weather instruments, some people used sayings such as "Ring around the sun, rain before night is done" to predict the weather. Even after the invention of weather instruments, there was no radio or television to get weather predictions to the people. Today, providing people with accurate weather predictions requires complicated instruments, sophisticated computer models, and up-to-date broadcasting equipment.

1. What are the following weather instruments used for? **(pages A16–A17)**

   home weather station _____

   pyrometer _____

2. On what facts are weather sayings based? Are any of them accurate? **(page A15)**

   _____
   _____
   _____
   _____
   _____

Section A • How's the Weather?

Workbook
Unit A • Weather Watch

Name_____ Date_____

Lesson 2 Summary (pages A18–A24)

As you read the summary, fill in the blanks with vocabulary terms from page A1. Then answer the questions that follow.

The sun is the most important factor in producing *weather*. The sun influences Earth's weather in two ways. First, Earth's land and water are warmed by the sun's energy. Because land heats and cools more quickly than water, the air above land heats and cools more quickly than the air above water. Warm air is less dense than cold air, so it rises. As warm air rises, it cools and becomes more dense. Then the cool, dense air sinks. The movement of air from places where it is dense to places where it is less dense is wind. Temperature differences between mountains and

valleys and between land and sea cause _____. There are general wind patterns also, caused by the movement of air between

the equator and the poles. These patterns are the _____.

1. Of all the sun's energy that reaches the Earth, none of it directly warms the air. What happens to the energy? **(page A19)**

   _____ % absorbed by ozone, clouds, and atmosphere

   _____ % reflected by surface

   _____ % absorbed by surface

   _____ % scattered and reflected by clouds and air

2. Name the three prevailing wind belts. **(page A24)**
   _____ _____ _____

3. Explain why the wind blows from the ocean toward the land on a summer day and from the land toward the ocean on a summer night. **(page A22)**

   _____
   _____
   _____
   _____
   _____
   _____

Name _____ Date _____

4. Use arrows to show the direction in which the wind is blowing in each of the examples of local winds shown below. **(page A22)**

Lesson 3 Summary (pages A25–A33)

As you read the summary, fill in the blanks with vocabulary terms from page A1. Then answer the questions that follow.

The second way in which the sun influences Earth's weather is through

the _____. As the sun warms the Earth's surface, water *evaporates* from the oceans into the air. The warmer the air, the more moisture it can hold. As the warm, moist air rises it cools, and the moisture *condenses*, forming fog or clouds. Clouds are of three basic types: cirrus, stratus, and cumulus. When cloud droplets or ice crystals

are too large to be suspended in air, they fall as _____.

1. Around what three kinds of particles does water vapor condense when moist air is cooled? **(page A29)**

   _____   _____   _____

2. Describe the conditions necessary for cloud formation. **(page A29)**

   _____
   _____
   _____
   _____
   _____

Name _____ Date _____

Lesson 4 Summary (pages A34–A37)

As you read the summary, fill in the blanks with vocabulary terms from page A1. Then answer the questions that follow.

A large body of air with the same temperature, pressure, and humidity is called an _____. Air masses are produced when air remains over one part of the Earth's surface for a long time. A _____, or boundary, forms between air masses. The passage of a front usually produces changes in temperature, pressure, wind speed and direction, and humidity.

1. What are three kinds of fronts that can form between air masses? **(page A37)**

   _____   _____   _____

2. Describe the air masses that affect the weather in the summer and in the winter where you live. **(pages A34–A35)**

   _____
   _____
   _____
   _____
   _____
   _____
   _____

3. Label each weather front below as a *warm front* or a *cold front*. **(page A37)**

   _____   _____

A4 Workbook
Unit A • Weather Watch   Section A • How's the Weather?

Name _____ Date _____

Lesson 5 Summary (pages A38–A45)

As you read the summary, fill in the blanks with vocabulary terms from page A1. Then answer the questions that follow.

Knowing what the weather will be helps everyone plan ahead. Weather predictions can be vital to farmers and truck drivers. Observations of changes in wind direction can be used to predict changes in weather. So, too, can changes in weather instruments, such as the

_____. A changing barometer, for example, means that

_____ is changing, which indicates that the weather will be changing soon. Newspapers and radio and TV stations provide a

daily weather prediction, or _____, of future weather.

1. How can a changing barometer be used to forecast weather changes? **(page A40)**

   _____

   _____

2. Using the data table on **page A43,** forecast what tomorrow's weather will be with each of the following weather conditions.

Weather Conditions	Forecast
North wind; barometer 28.56 and falling	
South wind; barometer 30.25 and steady	
East wind; barometer 29.99 and rising	
West wind; barometer 29.89 and rising	

3. Describe the weather changes that will occur if a warm, moist air mass now over your city is replaced by a cold, dry air mass. **(page A37)**

   _____

   _____

Name _____ Date _____

Review the Main Ideas

- Before there were accurate weather instruments, people predicted the weather by observing changes in nature. Some weather sayings are based on these observations.
- The sun heats the Earth unevenly. Uneven heating produces differences in air pressure that cause the wind to blow.
- The sun drives the water cycle. The sun evaporates water from the Earth's surface into the air, where water vapor condenses out, forming clouds and precipitation.
- When air remains over one part of the Earth's surface, an air mass forms. A boundary, or front, forms between air masses.
- Knowing what the weather will be helps people plan ahead. A weather forecast is a prediction of future weather.

Check the Vocabulary

Match the terms at the right with the definitions at the left.

____	1. a large body of air that has nearly the same temperature and moisture throughout	a. local winds
____	2. a prediction of future weather	b. front
____	3. water that falls from clouds in the form of rain, sleet, snow, or hail	c. air mass
____	4. global winds that blow mainly from one direction	d. prevailing winds
____	5. an instrument that measures air pressure	e. air pressure
____	6. winds that affect small areas	f. barometer
____	7. the force with which air pushes down on the Earth	g. precipitation
____	8. the process by which all the water on Earth is recycled	h. forecast
____	9. a boundary between air masses	i. water cycle

Name _____ Date _____

Storm Warning

SECTION B WORKBOOK

Science Concept
Certain weather conditions may lead to violent storms that can harm people and damage their property.

Vocabulary (pages A94–A95)

lightning	squall line	tornado
hurricane	blizzard	

Lesson 1 Summary (pages A47–A57)

As you read the summary, fill in the blank with a vocabulary term from above. Then answer the questions that follow.

As warm, moist air rises, it almost always produces storms with dark clouds, high winds, and heavy precipitation. Some storms become

severe, with thunder and _____, a huge electric spark that travels from cloud to cloud or from clouds to the ground. Lightning can be dangerous if a person or an object is in its path. In some thunderstorms, hail forms as rain freezes in the clouds and forms ice. If the precipitation is heavy enough or lasts long enough, flooding can occur.

Underline the best answer.

1. Precipitation that freezes high in the clouds is called . . .
   a. hail. **b.** sleet. **c.** snow. **(page A55)**

2. Lightning is caused by . . . **a.** a difference in charges between a cloud and the ground. **b.** clouds and the ground having the same charges. **c.** clouds and the ground having no charges. **(page A52)**

3. Describe the main characteristics of thunderstorms. **(page A48)**

_____
_____
_____
_____

Section B • Storm Warning

Workbook
Unit A • Weather Watch

Name _____ Date _____

4. Describe what is happening in each stage of thunderstorm development shown below. **(page A48)**

  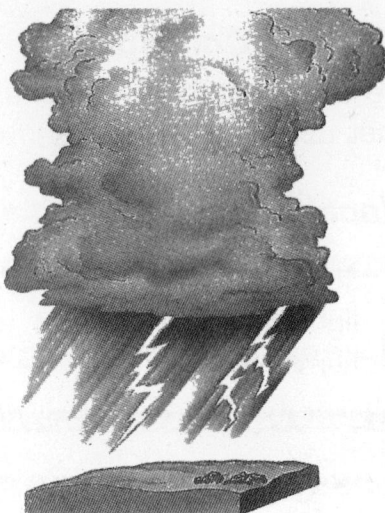

_____ _____ _____

_____ _____ _____

_____ _____ _____

Lesson 2 Summary (pages A58–A63)

As you read the summary, fill in the blanks with vocabulary terms from page A7. Then answer the questions that follow.

A line of violent thunderstorms, called a _____, sometimes accompanies the passage of a cold front. Warm air rises rapidly in front of the advancing cold air, producing an area of very low pressure. Air rushes into the low-pressure area from all sides, resulting in a twisting, funnel-shaped storm called a _____. The extremely high winds of a tornado can destroy almost everything in its path.

Underline the best answer.

1. Where warm and cold air masses meet . . .   **a.** it never rains.
   b. a squall line may form.   **c.** a hurricane may form. **(page A58)**

2. According to the table on **page A63**:

   Which state has the most tornadoes? _____

   Which state has the fewest tornadoes? _____

Name _____ Date _____

3. Describe the main characteristics of tornadoes. **(page A61)**

_____
_____
_____
_____
_____

Lesson 3 Summary (pages A64–A71)

As you read the summary, fill in the blanks with vocabulary terms from page A7. Then answer the questions that follow.

Over tropical oceans in summer months, conditions sometimes cause very warm, moist air to rise rapidly, forming a large, intense storm called a _____. A fully developed hurricane has bands of clouds spinning around a calm eye. As a hurricane nears land, strong winds, large waves, high tides, and torrential rains can cause extensive damage.

When cold air from the poles meets warm air from the tropics, a large spinning storm forms. In winter, these storms sometimes combine heavy snow and strong winds to produce a _____. Deep, drifting snow and bitter-cold temperatures make blizzards very dangerous.

Underline the best answer.

1. A hurricane may develop in ... **a.** a cold polar ocean. **b.** a warm tropical ocean. **c.** any ocean. **(page A66)**

2. A blizzard may develop where ... **a.** a polar air mass meets a cold, moist air mass. **b.** two warm air masses meet. **c.** a polar air mass meets a warm, moist air mass. **(page A70)**

3. Describe the main characteristics of blizzards. **(page A70)**

_____
_____
_____
_____

Name _____ Date _____

4. In the space below, draw a cross section of a hurricane. On your drawing, identify the *eye, prevailing winds,* and *downdraft.* Use arrows to show the movement of air in and around the hurricane. **(pages A66–A67)**

Name _____ Date _____

Review the Main Ideas

- Rising, moist air almost always produces storms; some storms can be severe, with thunder and lightning and heavy precipitation.
- A line of violent thunderstorms, or squall line, sometimes accompanies a cold front. Squall lines can even produce tornadoes.
- Hurricanes form over tropical oceans in summer months, and blizzards form in winter where cold, dry air meets warm, moist air.

Check the Vocabulary

Match the terms at the right with the definitions at the left.

___ 1. a small, severe storm that sometimes forms along squall lines	a. lightning
___ 2. a severe winter snowstorm	b. squall line
___ 3. a line of severe thunderstorms that forms along a strong cold front	c. tornado
___ 4. a giant tropical storm that can be very destructive because of damaging winds, heavy rains, and high waves	d. hurricane
___ 5. a huge electrical spark that jumps between clouds or from a cloud to the ground	e. blizzard

Name_____ Date_____

Different Places, Different Weather

SECTION C WORKBOOK

Science Concept
Climates are long-term weather patterns. Many factors cause climates to vary from place to place.

Vocabulary (pages A94–A95)

weather	climate	microclimate
greenhouse effect	global warming	

Lesson 1 Summary (pages A73–A78)

Read the summary, and then complete the concept map and answer the questions that follow.

The average weather of a particular place over a long period of time is known as *climate*. The climate of an area is determined by the air masses associated with its location on the Earth's surface. The climate of regions near the equator is *tropical* because of warm air masses. Cold air masses near the poles produce climates that are *polar*. The weather in tropical and polar climates remains stable throughout the year. Between the equator and the poles are regions with climates that are *temperate*. Temperate climates are affected by both warm and cold air masses at different times of the year, so the weather changes with the seasons.

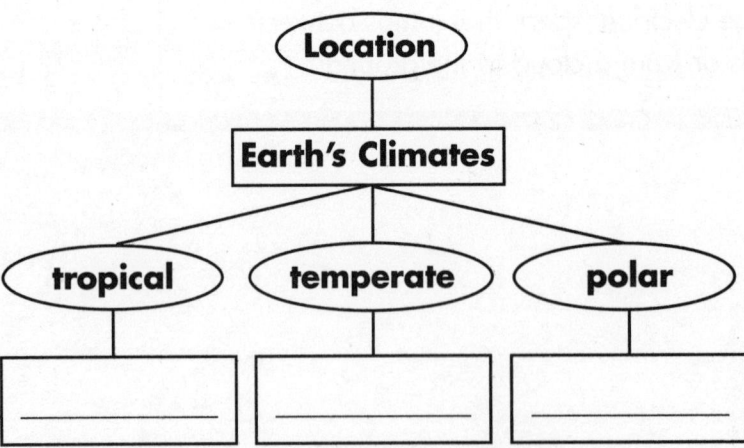

Name _____ Date _____

Read the descriptions of the major climatic zones, and then write the name of each. **(page A76)**

This climatic zone is located near the equator. In this zone, the average temperature in the coldest months is 18°C. This is higher than the average temperature of the warmest months in the polar zone.	The two regions of this climatic zone are located near the poles. In this zone, the warmest months average less than 10°C. This is lower than the average temperature of the coldest months in the tropical zone.	The two regions of this climatic zone are located between the climatic zone near the equator and the climatic zone located near each pole. The average temperature of the coldest months is lower than that of the tropical zone, while the average temperature of the warmest months is higher than that of the polar zone.
1. _____	2. _____	3. _____

4. How is today's weather related to the climate where you live? **(page A73)**

_____
_____
_____
_____

5. Label the polar, temperate, and tropical zones on this map.

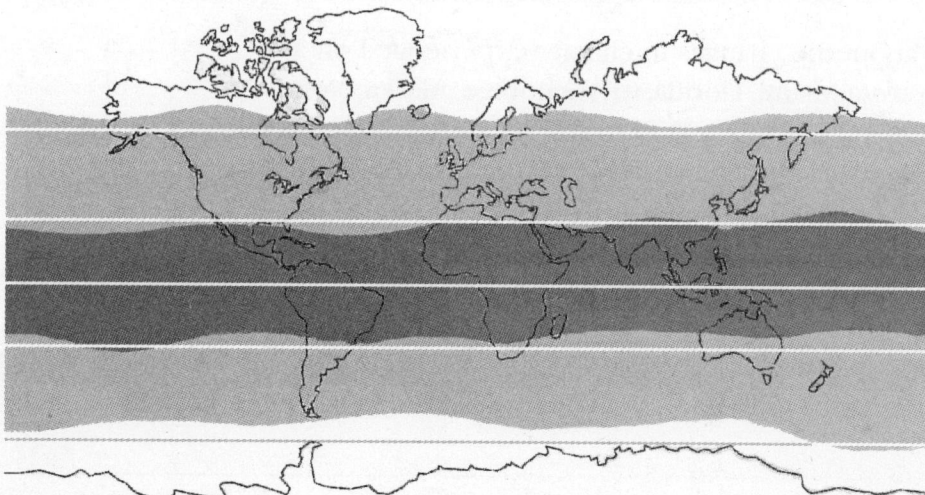

Section C • Different Places, Different Weather

Name_____ Date_____

Lesson 2 Summary (pages A79–A89)

As you read the summary, fill in the blanks with vocabulary terms from page A12. Then answer the questions that follow.

Local weather conditions often produce _____, areas whose climates are different from those of surrounding areas. Mountain shadows and heat islands are examples of microclimates. Large bodies of water and ocean currents tend to moderate climates. Altitude also affects climate. Going up a mountain is similar to traveling toward the poles—the climate generally gets colder. Human activity can also affect climate. The release of carbon dioxide from the burning of fuels

produces a _____, an increase in temperature.

A prolonged greenhouse effect could lead to _____, a permanent change in Earth's climates.

1. Show a rain shadow effect on the drawing below. Use arrows to show the prevailing winds. Then label the wet and the dry sides of the mountain. **(page A85)**

2. You have read about the changes in climate experienced on a November trip from Miami, Florida, to Anchorage, Alaska. Now suppose that you are taking a trip from the savanna of Zaire to the crest of the Ruwenzori Mountains. Describe the changes in climate as you climb the mountains. **(pages A86–A87)**

_____
_____
_____
_____
_____

Name _____ Date _____

3. In the space below, draw an example of a microclimate. **(page A78)**

4. Complete the following analogies based on the concept that part of an idea is related to the whole idea. **(pages A79–A87)**

Weather is to climate as greenhouse effect is to _____.

Temperature is to weather as _____ is to climate.

Review the Main Ideas

- The average weather of a particular place over a long period of time is known as climate. Earth's climates fall into three major types: polar, temperate, and tropical.
- Local weather conditions produce microclimates, such as rain shadows. Human activities can change climates, too. Global warming may be an effect of human activity.

Check the Vocabulary

Match the terms at the right with the definitions at the left.

___ 1. a process of trapping heat. Carbon dioxide and water vapor in the air trap heat, keeping the Earth warm.	a. climate
___ 2. the condition of the atmosphere	b. microclimate
___ 3. the climate of a small area	c. greenhouse effect
___ 4. a warming of climates around the world	d. global warming
___ 5. the average weather conditions over a long period of time	e. weather

Section C • Different Places, Different Weather

Name _____ Date _____

SECTION A WORKBOOK

Cells

Science Concept
Cells are the basic units of living things.

Vocabulary (pages B78–B79)

cell	cell membrane	cell theory
chloroplasts	chromosomes	cytoplasm
dehydration	diffusion	mitochondria
organelle	osmosis	nucleus

Lesson 1 Summary (pages B13–B15)

As you read the summary, fill in the blanks with vocabulary terms from above. Then answer the questions that follow.

Robert Hooke, working with a microscope in the 1600s, was the first scientist to identify and name the basic unit of living things—the

_____. Hooke's discovery led to the development of

the _____, with its three parts: First, all living things are made up of cells. Second, the cell is the smallest unit of structure and function in all living things. Third, all cells can reproduce to form new cells.

1. Who was the first person to use the term *cell*? **(page B14)** _____

2. In what material did he first see cells? **(page B14)** _____

3. What are the three parts of the cell theory? **(page B15)**

   a. _____

   b. _____

   c. _____

Section A • Cells

Unit B • The Inside Story

Name _____ Date _____

Lesson 2 Summary (pages B16–B18)

As you read the summary, fill in the blanks with vocabulary terms from page B1. Then complete the diagrams that follow.

Although cells are the basic units of living things, they are made up of many parts, each with a specific function. All cells are surrounded by a

_____ that controls what goes into and out of the cell.

The _____ is the command center of a cell. It controls everything that goes on inside the cell. Between the cell membrane and

the nucleus is a thick liquid called the _____. Suspended within the cytoplasm are other structures—organelles. An

_____ is any cell structure with a specific job to do. For

example, _____ supply a cell with the energy it needs.

1. Label the cell parts on the diagram below. **(page B17)**

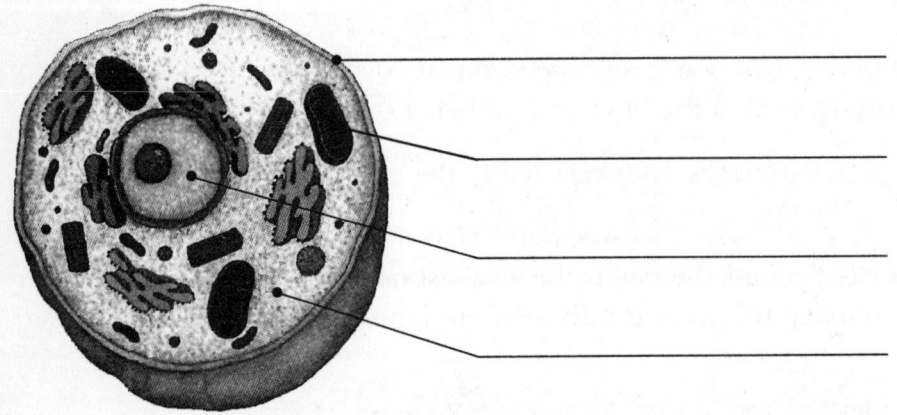

2. In the spaces below, draw a plant cell and an animal cell. Label the cell membrane, nucleus, and cytoplasm in each cell. Then draw and label the structures that make plant cells different from animal cells. **(page B18)**

Plant cell   Animal cell

Name _____ Date _____

Lesson 3 Summary (pages B19–B23)

As you read the summary, fill in the blanks with vocabulary terms from page B1. Then answer the questions that follow.

Cells need water, nutrients, and other materials to function. Some

materials move into and out of cells by _____, the movement of materials from an area with a lot of the material to an area with less of the material. Water moves across cell membranes by a kind

of diffusion called _____.

1. Fill in the blanks with the following terms that describe the movement of materials into and out of cells: *cell membrane, diffusion, nucleus, osmosis, dehydration.* **(pages B19–B23)**

   _____ is the movement of materials from an area that has a lot of the material to an area that has less of the material.

   _____ happens when cells lose more water than they take in.

   _____ is the diffusion of water through a cell membrane.

   The _____ controls the movement of materials, since it controls all the activities of a cell.

   The _____ selects what passes into and out of a cell.

2. Explain what happens to the cells of your body if you sweat a lot but do not drink enough water. **(page B19)**

   _____
   _____
   _____
   _____

Name _____ Date _____

3. Explain what happens when you water a wilted plant. **(page B23)**

_____
_____
_____
_____

Lesson 4 Summary (pages B24–B27)

As you read the summary, fill in the blanks with vocabulary terms from page B1. (Note: Some terms may be used more than once.) Then answer the questions that follow.

Within the _____ of a cell are thin strands called

_____, which contain the instructions for controlling all the functions of the cell. Before a cell divides, it makes an exact copy of

the _____. During cell division, the _____

and the _____ of the cell divide so that each new

cell receives a full set of _____ and half the

_____ of the original cell.

Reread the "Cell Theory Rap" on **pages B26–B27,** *and then answer the following questions about the functions of additional cell organelles.*

1. What organelle surrounds and protects the nucleus? _____

2. What organelles act as protein factories for the cells? _____

3. What organelle carries materials to and from the membrane?

_____

4. What organelles carry food and water throughout a cell? _____

Name _____ Date _____

5. In the boxes below, draw a cell with two chromosomes, and show what happens to the chromosomes during cell division. **(page B24)**

Review the Main Ideas

- Robert Hooke was the first person to identify and name the basic unit of living things—the cell. His discovery led to the development of the cell theory.
- Although cells are the basic units of all living things, they are made up of many parts—organelles—each with a specific function.
- Cells need water, nutrients, and other materials to function. Materials move into and out of a cell across the cell membrane.
- The instructions for controlling a cell are contained within chromosomes. Before a cell divides, it makes an exact copy of the chromosomes.

Name _____ Date _____

Check the Vocabulary

Match the terms at the right with the definitions at the left.

____	1. one of the major theories of life science	a. cell
____	2. the movement of a material into an area that has less of the material	b. cell membrane
____	3. loss of water	c. cell theory
____	4. organelles that make food in plant cells	d. chloroplasts
____	5. the living material between a cell's nucleus and its cell membrane	e. chromosomes
____	6. the basic unit of structure and function in an organism	f. cytoplasm
____	7. structures in the nucleus of a cell that contain the instructions that enable the nucleus to control the activities of the cell	g. dehydration
____	8. organelles that produce the energy a cell needs	h. diffusion
____	9. a protective covering around a cell	i. mitochondria
____	10. the control center of a cell	j. organelle
____	11. any cell structure that has a specific job to do	k. osmosis
____	12. the diffusion of water through a cell membrane	l. nucleus

Name _____ Date _____

SECTION B WORKBOOK

We're Organized

Science Concept
Every living thing is the sum of its parts.

Vocabulary (pages B78–B79)

cell	organ	organism
system	tissues	blood

Lesson 1 Summary (pages B29–B37)

As you read the summary, fill in the blanks with vocabulary terms from above. Then complete the table that follows.

The _____ is the first of five levels of organization of living things. Groups of cells that have the same structure and do the same job are called _____. The muscle in your biceps—in the front of your arm—is an example of a tissue. An _____ is a group of different kinds of tissues working together to do a specific job. Your heart is an example of an organ. A _____ is a group of organs working together to do a job. Your respiratory system, for example, is responsible for breathing. Your entire body is an example of the highest level of organization—the _____.

Classify each thing listed below by using one of these terms: cell, tissue, organ, system, organism.

_____	stomach	_____	muscle
_____	blood	_____	lung
_____	leaf	_____	oak tree
_____	digestive	_____	nervous
_____	nerve	_____	tibia
_____	tree bark	_____	amoeba

Name _____ Date _____

Lesson 2 Summary (pages B38–B49)

Read the summary, and then complete the table.

Blood is a tissue composed of several kinds of cells—red blood cells, white blood cells, and platelets. Blood is part of a body system that includes several major organs, such as the heart.

Your body has trillions of cells, hundreds of tissues, dozens of organs, and ten systems: skeletal system, muscular system, digestive system, nervous system, excretory system, respiratory system, circulatory system, endocrine system, reproductive system, and integumentary system.

System	Function
_____	This system transports materials to all parts of your body.
_____	Without this system, you couldn't move from place to place or lift things.
_____	This system regulates growth and development and helps control some body functions.
_____	Bones of this system give your body its shape and provide support. They also protect internal organs.
_____	The skin, hair, and nails of this system provide a protective layer for your body.
_____	This system provides a way for adults to produce offspring.
_____	This system takes in oxygen and releases carbon dioxide.
_____	The food you eat must be broken down by this system into nutrients your body cells can use.
_____	This system removes the wastes produced by your body cells.
_____	This system controls your body and helps you respond to your environment.

Answer the following questions about blood. **(page B39)**

1. The solid part of blood is mostly _____.

2. The liquid part of blood, which is mostly water, is called _____.

3. Protection from disease and infection is provided by _____.

4. The flow of blood from a cut is slowed and stopped by _____.

Name _____ Date _____

5. Describe how the digestive system, the circulatory system, and the respiratory system work together to provide your body cells with the food and oxygen they need to function. **(pages B45–B47)**

_____
_____
_____
_____
_____
_____

Review the Main Ideas

- Cells are the basic units of all living things. Groups of cells with the same function are called tissues.
- Groups of tissues with the same function are called organs. Organs with related functions belong to a system.

Check the Vocabulary

Match the terms at the right with the definitions at the left.

____ 1.	a body structure made of different kinds of tissues that work together to do a specific job	a. cell
____ 2.	groups of cells with the same structure and function	b. tissues
____ 3.	the basic unit of structure and function of an organism	c. organ
____ 4.	fluid tissue that moves from place to place	d. system
____ 5.	a living thing that carries out all life functions	e. organism
____ 6.	a group of organs that work together to do a job	f. blood

Name_____ Date_____

SECTION C WORKBOOK

In Sickness and in Health

Science Concept
The human body has specialized cells that fight disease-causing organisms.

Vocabulary (pages B78–B79)

| antibodies | antibiotics | antiseptics |

Lesson 1 Summary (pages B51–B54)

Read the summary, and then answer the questions that follow.

There are germs around you that can be seen only with a microscope. Some of these can cause diseases. Germs such as the viruses that cause colds and influenza can be spread by direct touch or by coughing and sneezing. It is hard to avoid these germs. Other germs, such as the virus that causes AIDS, can be passed only by specific acts. It is easier to avoid this germ.

1. Name three ways that the germs that cause colds can be spread. **(pages B52–B53)**
   _____ _____ _____

2. What is a fever? **(page B54)**
   _____

Lesson 2 Summary (pages B55–B65)

As you read the summary, fill in the blanks with these terms: viruses, bacteria, protozoa, fungi. *Then answer the questions that follow.*

Several kinds of microorganisms cause diseases. Some microorganisms can live and reproduce on their own, but others are parasites and need a host. A host is an organism on which or in which a parasite lives or reproduces. Many familiar diseases, such as strep throat and tetanus, are

caused by _____. Malaria and African sleeping sickness

are caused by _____, while _____ cause ringworm and athlete's foot.

B10 Workbook
Unit B • The Inside Story

Section C • In Sickness and in Health

Name _____ Date _____

Diseases can also be caused by _____, which are not microorganisms. Remember, all organisms are made up of cells, and _____ aren't made up of cells. They can reproduce, however, by taking over a host. Diseases such as colds, chicken pox, influenza, and AIDS are caused by _____.

1. Describe two different parasites and the diseases they cause. **(pages B62–B63)**

   _____
   _____
   _____
   _____
   _____
   _____

2. From the diagrams below, describe what is happening in each stage of the infection of a host cell by a virus. **(page B60)**

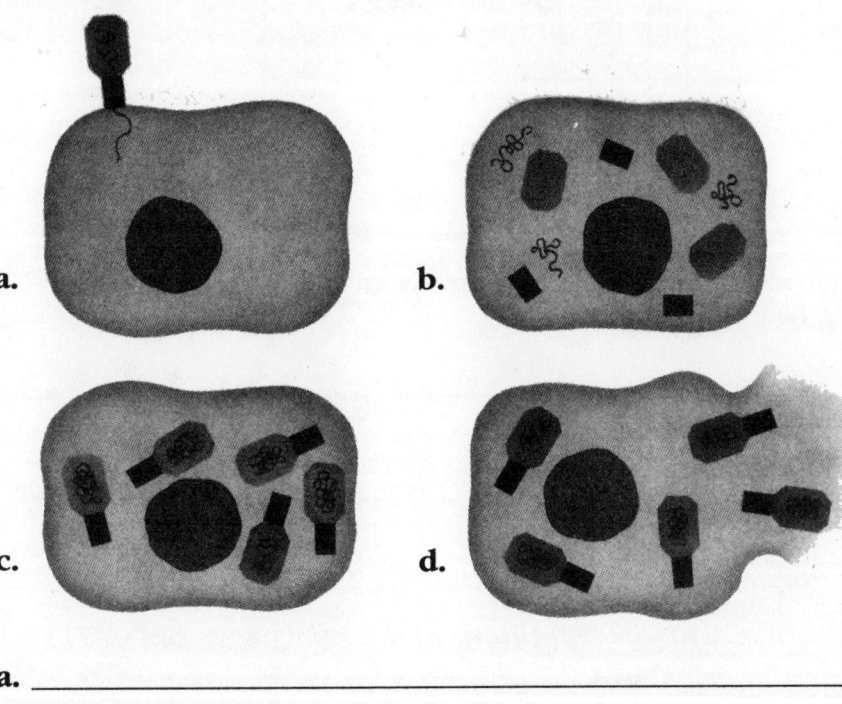

   a. _____
   b. _____
   c. _____
   d. _____

Section C • In Sickness and in Health

Workbook
Unit B • The Inside Story   B11

Name_____ Date_____

Lesson 3 Summary (pages B66–B73)

As you read the summary, fill in the blanks with vocabulary terms from page B10. Then answer the questions that follow.

Your body has many natural defenses against diseases. For example, the passages of your respiratory system are coated with mucus—a thick,

sticky substance that traps microorganisms. _____ and white blood cells in your circulatory system seek out and destroy parasites. Vaccinations provide artificial immunity against certain diseases. Disease-causing organisms can also be stopped or destroyed by

_____ and other chemicals called _____.

1. Complete the concept map. **(pages B60–B71)**

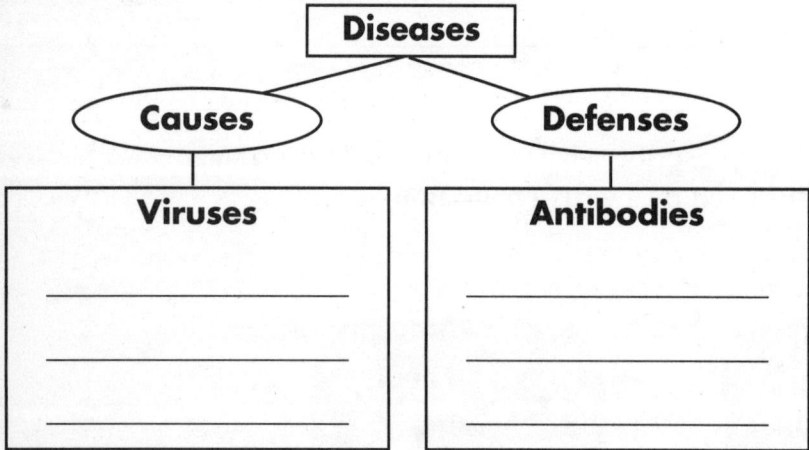

2. Describe two of the body's natural defenses against invading microorganisms. **(pages B66–B67)**

_____
_____
_____
_____

Match the terms at the right with the definitions at the left. **(pages B66–B71)**

____ 3. chemicals that keep bacteria from growing	**a.** antibodies
____ 4. proteins in your body that destroy or weaken microorganisms	**b.** antiseptics
____ 5. strong chemicals that kill bacteria	**c.** antibiotics

Name _____ Date _____

Review the Main Ideas

- There are viruses and microorganisms all around us; some of them can cause diseases.
- Colds and influenza are caused by viruses. Strep throat is caused by bacteria. Malaria is caused by protozoa, and fungi cause athlete's foot.
- The body has some natural defenses against diseases. Certain medicines and chemicals can also help fight diseases.

Check the Facts

Underline the best answer.

1. Colds are caused by... **a.** bacteria. **b.** viruses. **c.** protozoa. **(page B60)**

2. Bacteria can be killed by... **a.** antibiotics. **b.** antiseptics. **c.** antigens. **(page B70)**

3. Bacteria are different from other cells in that bacteria have... **a.** no nucleus. **b.** no membranes. **c.** extra cytoplasm. **(page B56)**

4. The bacteria that cause strep throat are... **a.** rod-shaped. **b.** spiral-shaped. **c.** round. **(page B58)**

5. Unlike bacteria, most protozoa... **a.** can move. **b.** are round. **c.** cannot be killed. **(page B62)**

6. Ringworm is caused by... **a.** bacteria. **b.** fungi. **c.** protozoa. **(page B63)**

7. Microorganisms in the blood stream can be killed by... **a.** antiseptics. **b.** antiagents. **c.** antibodies. **(page B67)**

8. Some antibodies are made naturally, while others are acquired through... **a.** vaccinations. **b.** friends. **c.** physicians. **(page B67)**

9. Sir Alexander Fleming developed the first... **a.** antiseptic. **b.** antibiotic. **c.** antiviral. **(page B71)**

10. All of the following are natural defenses against disease except... **a.** mucus. **b.** antibodies. **c.** antiseptics. **(page B66)**

Name _____ Date _____

Going Around Together

SECTION A WORKBOOK

Science Concept

StarBase Earth is an observatory from which people can learn about the universe.

Vocabulary (pages C94–C96)

astronomers	eclipse	solstice
orbit	rotation	equinox
ellipse	revolution	phases
gravity	moon	crater

Lesson 1 Summary (pages C13–C23)

As you read the summary, fill in the blanks with vocabulary terms from above. Then answer the questions that follow.

Although ancient people had no telescopes, they were careful

_____, or observers of the universe. They built elaborate observatories, such as Stonehenge and El Caracol. These early people observed the regular patterns of the universe and even discovered that

the Earth and other planets circle, or _____, the sun. Some of their earliest observations were about Earth's closest neighbor

in space, the _____.

Ancient astronomers first observed the "face" in the moon. They also

tried to predict the next occurrence of a solar _____, when the moon's shadow passes over the Earth. In the 1600s, Sir Isaac Newton wondered why the moon didn't just fly off into space. He finally decided that all bodies in the universe are attracted to each

other. This attraction is called _____.

1. Who first calculated the distance from the Earth to the sun? He was also the first scientist who said that the Earth and the other planets orbit around the sun. **(page C16)**

_____

Section A • *Going Around Together*

Workbook
Unit C • StarBase Earth   C1

Name _____ Date _____

2. Who came up with the law of universal gravitation? He also had a problem with things falling on his head. **(pages C20–C21)**

   _____

3. What early people thought eclipses were fights between the sun and the moon? **(page C23)**

   _____

4. Describe the position of the Earth, the moon, and the sun during a solar eclipse. **(pages C22–C23)**

   _____
   _____
   _____
   _____

5. Describe the position of the Earth, the moon, and the sun during a lunar eclipse. **(pages C22–C23)**

   _____
   _____
   _____
   _____

6. In the space below, make a drawing that shows the Earth in orbit around the sun, and the moon in orbit around the Earth. **(page C21)**

Workbook
Unit C • StarBase Earth

Section A • Going Around Together

Name _____ Date _____

Lesson 2 Summary (pages C24–C31)

As you read the summary, fill in the blanks with vocabulary terms from page C1. (Some of the terms may be used more than once.) Then answer the questions that follow.

Like the early astronomers, who observed the periodic changes, or

_____, of the moon, you, too, can observe many things about the Earth, the moon, and the sun. For example, you can observe

that Earth's _____ on its axis causes the cycle of day and night, and that the cycle of seasons is caused by Earth's

_____ around the sun. You can observe also that the

orbit of the Earth around the sun is an _____ rather than a perfect circle and that the tilt of the Earth on its axis results in days and nights of different lengths, depending on the season. The

longest and shortest days are the summer _____ and

winter _____, while the days of equal light and dark are

the spring _____ and the fall _____.

1. What group of people preserved many astronomical records during the Middle Ages? They also developed an instrument for measuring the altitude of the sun and the stars. **(page C24)**

   _____

2. In what European country are the people always delighted by the appearance of the northern lights during the long winter nights? **(page C29)**

   _____

3. What are the names of the especially high and low tides and the moderate tides that occur during each moon cycle? **(page C31)**

   _____

4. Explain what causes the phases of the moon. **(page C30)**

   _____

   _____

   _____

   _____

Name_____ Date_____

5. On the diagram below, identify, label, and date the positions of the following: *summer solstice, winter solstice, spring equinox,* and *fall equinox.* **(page C28)**

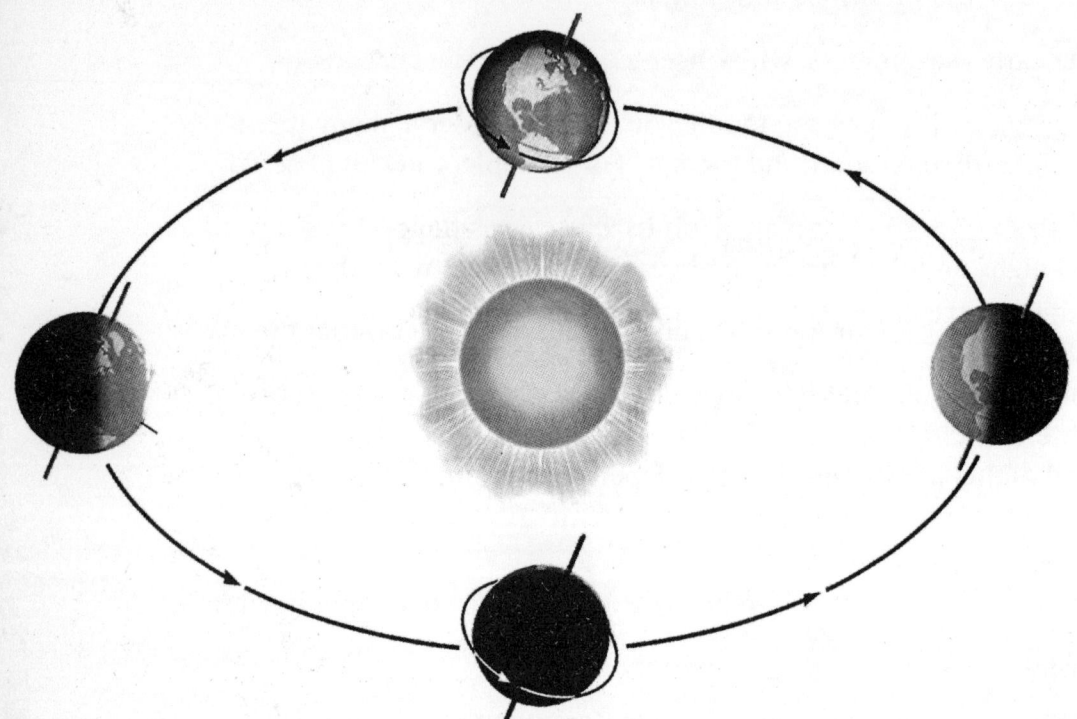

Lesson 3 Summary (pages C32–C35)

Read the summary, and then answer the questions that follow.

On July 20, 1969, humans first explored the moon. They found that the moon has practically no atmosphere and that temperatures vary wildly from day to night. The moon is about the same age as Earth, and scientists hypothesize that it may have once been part of Earth. There is evidence of volcanoes, and much of the moon's surface is covered with large craters, from rocks impacting its surface.

1. Who were the first humans to stand on the surface of the moon? One of them remarked that it was "...one small step...." **(pages C32–C33)**

_____

Name _____ Date _____

2. Describe three ways that scientists determine the relative ages of features on the moon. **(page C34)**

_____

_____

_____

Review the Main Ideas

- Ancient astronomers made many observations of the sun, the moon, and the planets.
- Some of the earliest observations of astronomers centered on Earth's rotation on its axis and its revolution around the sun.

Check the Vocabulary

Match the terms at the right with the definitions at the left.

___ 1. a flattened circle	a. astronomer
___ 2. movement of one object around another	b. orbit
___ 3. force of attraction between particles of matter	c. ellipse
___ 4. the spinning of a body about its axis	d. gravity
___ 5. a scientist who studies the planets, stars, and other celestial objects	e. eclipse
___ 6. a temporary blocking out of the moon (by the sun) or the sun (by the moon)	f. rotation
___ 7. days with the most hours of daylight or the fewest hours of daylight	g. revolution
___ 8. path one object takes around another	h. solstice
___ 9. a deep impression left on the surface of a planet or moon by the impact of a rock	i. equinox
___ 10. days with equal periods of day and night	j. phase
___ 11. one of the apparent shapes of the moon	k. crater

Section A • Going Around Together

Workbook
Unit C • StarBase Earth   C5

Name _____ Date _____

SECTION B WORKBOOK

Close to Home

Science Concept
The bodies in StarBase Earth's solar system have major similarities and differences.

Vocabulary (pages C94–C96)

solar system	planet	satellite
astronomical unit	asteroids	comets
meteor	meteorite	meteoroids

Lesson 1 Summary (pages C37–C40)

As you read the summary, fill in the blanks with vocabulary terms from above. Then identify the objects in the diagram that follows.

Earth is the third _____ from the sun. The

_____ can be divided into the inner planets and the outer planets. The inner planets include Mercury, Venus, Earth, and Mars. The outer planets include Jupiter, Saturn, Uranus, Neptune, and Pluto. Because distances in the solar system are so great, astronomers use a

measurement called an AU, or _____, which is the distance between the Earth and the sun.

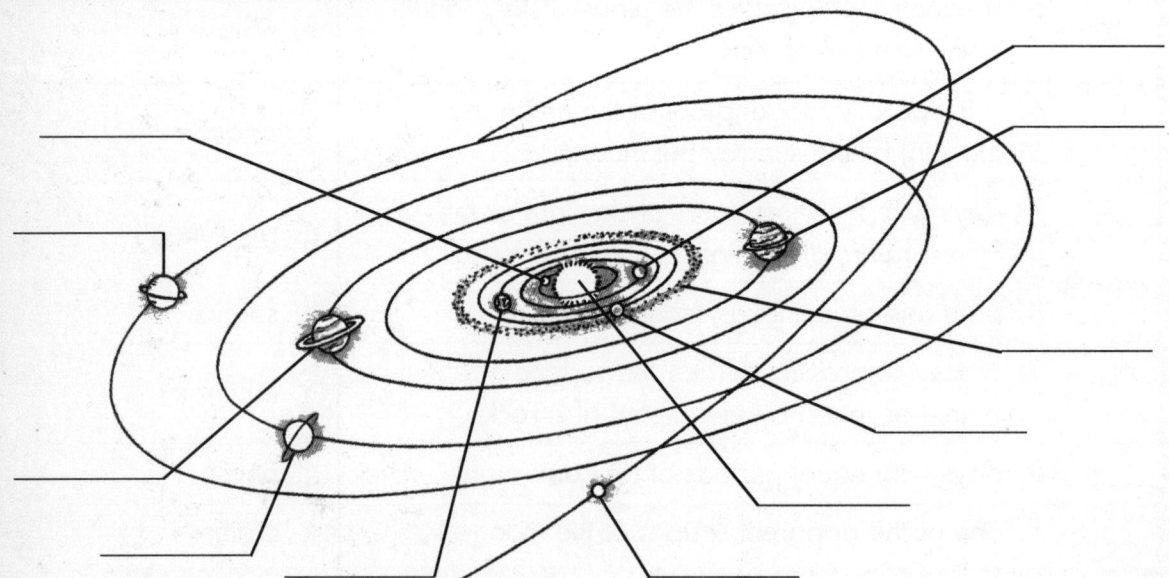

Workbook
C6   Unit C • StarBase Earth

Section B • Close to Home

Name _____ Date _____

Lesson 2 Summary (pages C41–C45)

As you read the summary, fill in the blanks with vocabulary terms from page C6. Then answer the questions that follow.

Mercury is the planet closest to the sun. It is about the size of Earth's moon. Mercury's surface is rocky, and the planet has little or no atmosphere. Venus, the second planet from the sun, is about the size of Earth. Venus has a rocky surface and a hot, thick atmosphere. Earth, the third planet from the sun, has a rocky surface and is mostly covered with water. Earth's atmosphere keeps the temperature moderate and supports life. Earth is the first planet from the sun to have a moon, or

_____. Mars, the fourth planet from the sun, is about half the size of Earth. Mars has a rocky surface, a thin atmosphere, and two moons. Between the inner planets and the outer planets is a belt of

_____, containing thousands of large pieces of rock, which may be part of an unformed planet.

Choose the correct planet for the following questions.

1. Which planet has an oxygen-rich atmosphere, oceans, and a greenhouse effect that supports life? **(page C42)** _____

2. Which planet has a dense, hot atmosphere containing carbon dioxide and sulfuric acid? **(page C41)** _____

3. Which planet has mountains, deserts, volcanoes, canyons, and a thin atmosphere of carbon dioxide? **(page C44)** _____

4. Which planet is too small for its gravity to hold onto an atmosphere or a moon? **(page C41)** _____

5. Explain why the asteroids may be parts of a planet that never formed. **(page C45)**

_____
_____
_____
_____

Name _____ Date _____

Lesson 3 Summary (pages C46–C53)

As you read the summary, fill in the blanks with vocabulary terms from page C6. Then complete the table and answer the questions that follow.

Jupiter, the fifth planet from the sun, is larger than all the other planets combined. Most of Jupiter is a thick, swirling mass of clouds. Jupiter has 17 moons and a small, thin ring. Saturn, the sixth planet from the sun, is similar to Jupiter, but much smaller. Saturn has a much larger ring system than Jupiter. Uranus and Neptune, the seventh and eighth planets, are also similar to Jupiter and Saturn. Pluto, the last planet from the sun, is very different from the other outer planets. It is rocky and very small. Pluto has one moon, Charon.

Also orbiting the sun are _____, chunks of ice and rock left over from the formation of the solar system. Comets leave behind a trail of gas and dust, or _____. As Earth passes through this dust, the particles stream into our atmosphere as a _____. If a large chunk, a _____, survives, it may strike the Earth.

Inner Planets	Outer Planets
_____	_____
_____	_____
_____	_____
Asteroids	_____

Choose the correct planet for the following questions.

1. Which planet has a giant red spot that may be a huge storm? **(page C47)** _____

2. Which planet could float on water? **(page C48)** _____

3. Which planet has white clouds of methane ice and a moon nicknamed "the cantaloupe moon"? **(page C51)** _____

4. Which planet has a moon nearly half its size and is sometimes called a double planet? **(page C51)** _____

5. Which planet is blue-green? **(page C51)** _____

6. Explain the relationship among meteors, meteorites, and meteoroids. **(page C53)**

_____
_____
_____
_____

7. Describe how astronomers discovered Neptune and Pluto. **(page C49)**

_____
_____
_____
_____
_____
_____

Lesson 4 Summary (pages C54–C55)

Read the summary, and then answer the questions that follow.

For more than 30 years, scientists have been trying to find other forms of life in the solar system and beyond. Since 1992, a full-scale program called SETI (Search for ExtraTerrestrial Intelligence) has been carried out, using radio channels all over the Earth.

1. What four kinds of information are found on the SETI message? **(page C54)**

   _____   _____

   _____   _____

2. Where is the world's largest radiotelescope located? **(page C54)**

   _____

3. When did astronomers begin the search for extraterrestrial life? **(page C54)**

   _____

Name_____   Date_____

Review the Main Ideas

- The solar system can be divided into the inner planets—Mercury, Venus, Earth, and Mars—and the outer planets—Jupiter, Saturn, Uranus, Neptune, and Pluto. In addition, asteroids orbit the sun between Mars and Jupiter, and comets circle the sun in long, oval-shaped orbits.
- Generally, the inner planets have rocky surfaces, while the outer planets—with the exception of Pluto—are giant balls of gases.
- Scientists have been looking for other forms of life in the solar system, but conditions that led to life on Earth are rare outside of our planet.

Check the Vocabulary

Match the terms at the right with the definitions at the left.

____ 1. the distance between the Earth and the sun	a. solar system
____ 2. chunks of ice and rock that travel around the sun in a variety of orbits	b. astronomical unit
____ 3. a meteoroid that enters Earth's atmosphere	c. meteor
____ 4. one of the nine large, nearly round objects revolving around the sun	d. planet
____ 5. a natural or artificial body that orbits another body	e. asteroids
____ 6. the sun, its family of planets, and all the asteroids, comets, and meteoroids	f. meteorite
____ 7. small, rocky bodies that orbit the sun between the orbits of Mars and Jupiter	g. satellite
____ 8. dust, gas particles, and rocks thrown off by comets	h. comets
____ 9. a meteor that plunges to Earth in one piece	i. meteoroids

Name _____ Date _____

Stars Above

SECTION C WORKBOOK

Science Concept
From our position on StarBase Earth, we can use both our eyes and technological tools to explore the universe.

Vocabulary (pages C94–C96)

axis	circumpolar	constellations
galaxy	light-years	star
telescope	universe	

Lesson 1 Summary (pages C57–C61)

As you read the summary, fill in the blanks with vocabulary terms from above. Then answer the questions that follow.

To someone on StarBase Earth, each _____ looks as if it is attached to the inside of a huge ball. Astronomers call this ball the

celestial sphere. Since the Earth rotates on its _____ from west to east, the celestial sphere seems to rotate from east to west, so most stars seem to rise in the east and set in the west, like the sun.

However, some stars, called _____ stars, are always above the horizon.

Throughout the year, different star patterns, or _____, appear on the celestial sphere. Ancient astronomers noted that the sun seemed to move through the same constellations year after year. They named this path the ecliptic. The 12 constellations that lie on the path of the ecliptic are called the zodiac.

Underline the best answer.

1. The 12 constellations that lie on the path of the ecliptic are also known as the ... **a.** universe. **b.** zodiac. **c.** celestial sphere. **(page C61)**

2. Although many people refer to it as such, the Big Dipper is not really a ... **a.** star chart. **b.** constellation. **c.** zodiac. **(page C61)**

Section C • Stars Above

Workbook
Unit C • StarBase Earth C11

Name _____ Date _____

3. Many stars appear to rise in the east and set in the west, but the North star remains above the horizon because it is ... **a.** fixed. **b.** circumpolar. **c.** a constellation. **(page C59)**

4. Observers often say that certain constellations rise in the east and set in the west, but this is not what really happens. Explain what really happens. **(page C57)**

_____

_____

_____

_____

Lesson 2 Summary (pages C62–C68)

Read the summary, and then answer the questions that follow.

Early astronomers made observations of the stars with their unaided eyes. In 1609 Galileo used a simple *refracting telescope* (a telescope that uses two lenses to gather and focus light) to observe the universe. Sixty years later, Sir Isaac Newton invented a *reflecting telescope* (a telescope that uses mirrors to gather and focus light). Most large telescopes today, including the world's largest, are reflecting telescopes. Although not the largest, the Hubble Space Telescope can make some of the best observations of distant stars from its position above the Earth's atmosphere.

Underline the best answer.

1. The type of telescope Newton invented was the ...
   a. radio telescope. **b.** reflecting telescope. **c.** refracting telescope. **(page C64)**

2. The type of telescope through which Galileo first observed moons orbiting around Jupiter was a ... **a.** radio telescope. **b.** reflecting telescope. **c.** refracting telescope. **(page C64)**

3. The largest telescope in the world is the Keck I telescope on Mauna Kea in ... **a.** Alaska. **b.** Hawai'i. **c.** Wisconsin. **(page C67)**

4. The Hubble Space Telescope is a ... **a.** radio telescope. **b.** reflecting telescope. **c.** refracting telescope. **(page C68)**

Name _____ Date _____

5. Identify each telescope in the diagram, and then describe the similarities and the differences between reflecting telescopes and refracting telescopes. **(page C64)**

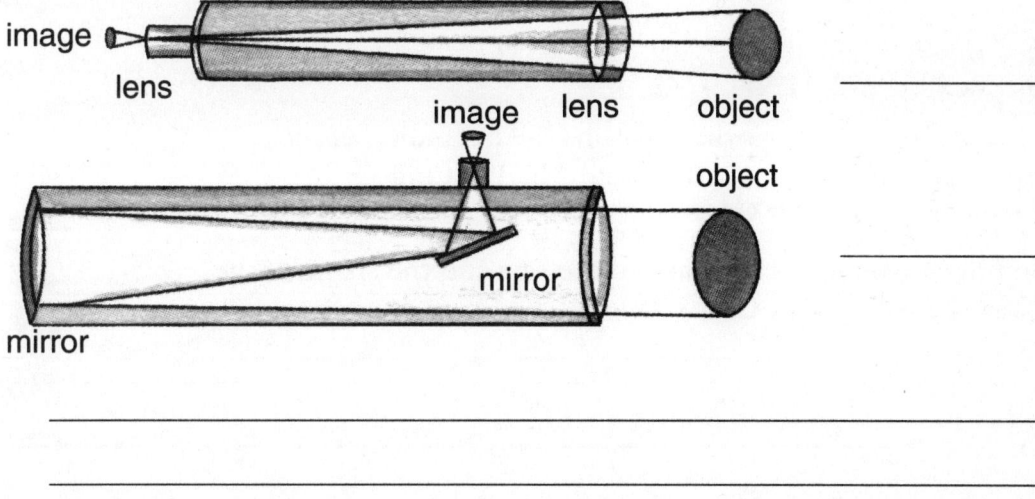

_____

_____

_____
_____
_____
_____
_____
_____
_____

Lesson 3 Summary (pages C69–C73)

As you read the summary, fill in the blanks with vocabulary terms from page C11. Then answer the questions that follow.

Many scientists hypothesize that 15 billion years ago, all matter in

the _____ was squeezed into a tiny, hot point. Then, suddenly, this matter began to expand outward, as if a giant explosion had occurred. It is still expanding today.

Since distances even within our own _____ are so great, astronomers measure distances in _____, rather than in astronomical units (a light-year is the distance light travels in a year). The Milky Way Galaxy measures about 100,000 light-years from end to end, is about 10,000 light-years across, and contains about 200 billion stars. The closest neighboring galaxy—Andromeda—is about 2.3 million light-years away.

Name _____ Date _____

Underline the best answer.

1. The "Backbone of Night" is another name for the . . .   **a.** Big Dipper.
   b. Milky Way Galaxy.   **c.** North Star. **(page C69)**

2. Galaxy M104 is nicknamed the . . .   **a.** Big Dipper.   **b.** Sombrero Galaxy.   **c.** Big Bang. **(page C72)**

3. A good name for the theory that explains the beginning of the universe might be the . . .   **a.** Big Bang.   **b.** Big Chill.   **c.** Big Squeeze. **(page C73)**

4. Explain how astronomers determined the size and the shape of the Milky Way Galaxy. **(pages C71–C72)**

   _____
   _____
   _____
   _____

5. In the space below, draw and label a side view and a top view of the Milky Way Galaxy. **(page C71)**

Name _____ Date _____

Review the Main Ideas

- From Earth, the stars seem to be attached to the inside of the celestial sphere. Throughout the year, constellations rise in the east and set in the west, like the sun.
- Early astronomers made observations of the night sky without the aid of telescopes. Galileo was one of the first to use a refracting telescope to study the stars and planets, while Sir Isaac Newton invented a reflecting telescope to help him study the stars.
- Scientists hypothesize that the universe began with a "big bang" about 15 billion years ago. Although the universe is still expanding, clumps of matter have slowed down and formed galaxies like our own Milky Way Galaxy.

Check the Vocabulary

Match the terms at the right with the definitions at the left.

____ 1. a large globe of hot gas, shining by its own light	a. constellation
____ 2. around the poles	b. light-year
____ 3. an imaginary line around which a planet rotates	c. axis
____ 4. the distance light travels in a year	d. galaxy
____ 5. a device that makes distant objects appear larger, brighter, and more detailed	e. universe
____ 6. a vast collection of stars	f. star
____ 7. everything there is—all the stars, solar systems, galaxies, dust, gas—all matter	g. telescope
____ 8. a group of stars that appear to make a picture of some sort in the night sky	h. circumpolar

Section C • Stars Above

Workbook
Unit C • StarBase Earth

Name _____ Date _____

Stars Near and Far

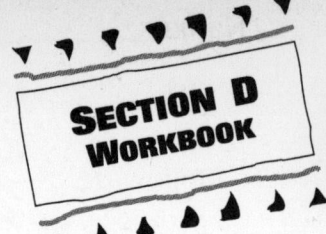

Science Concept

The sun and all the other stars in the universe can be classified according to their characteristics.

Vocabulary (pages C94–C96)

| core | corona | magnitude |

Lesson 1 Summary (pages C75–C79)

As you read the summary, fill in the blanks with vocabulary terms from above. Then answer the questions that follow.

Earth's nearest star—the sun—is about 1.4 billion kilometers in diameter. Like all stars, the sun is a glowing globe of hot gas. The hydrogen at the sun's _____ is compressed and heated by the weight of its outer layers to a temperature of 14 million° C. Its _____, or atmosphere, is a cool 2 million° C. The sun, like all the other stars in the universe, is a source of tremendous energy.

1. The part of the sun that is visible is called the _____. **(page C76)**

2. Areas of the sun that are cooler than the rest of the sun's surface are called _____. **(page C77)**

3. Fast-moving particles given off by the sun's corona become the _____. **(page C79)**

4. Explain how energy produced in the core of the sun travels through the sun to its surface. **(pages C76–C77)**

_____
_____
_____
_____

Name _____ Date _____

5. In the space below, draw a diagram of the sun, and identify the following: *photosphere, radiative layer, convective layer, core, solar prominences, corona, sunspots, chromosphere.* **(pages C76–C77)**

Lesson 2 Summary (pages C80–C85)

As you read the summary, fill in the blank with a vocabulary term from page C16. Then answer the questions that follow.

Stars release energy as gamma rays, X rays, ultraviolet waves, microwaves, and radio waves, as well as the more obvious heat and light. It is the light, or brightness, of distant stars that makes them visible

from StarBase Earth. Astronomers use _____ to refer to a star's brightness, although a star's *apparent magnitude* depends more on its distance from Earth than on its size. *Absolute magnitude* is a better measure of a star's brightness. Absolute magnitude is a measure of a star's size, mass, color, and temperature.

1. _____ can be used to detect heat sources. **(page C83)**

2. _____ waves from the sun can cause sunburn. **(page C84)**

3. _____ from the sun are similar to the ones used to cook food quickly. **(page C85)**

Name_____ Date_____

4. Explain the difference between apparent magnitude and absolute magnitude. **(pages C81–C82)**

_____
_____
_____
_____

5. In the space below, make a graph that shows the various waves of energy produced by stars. **(pages C84–C85)**

Lesson 3 Summary (pages C86–C89)

Read the summary. Then label the diagram and answer the questions that follow.

Since absolute magnitude is a measure of a star's size, mass, color, and temperature, these properties can be used to classify stars. The sun is average, as stars go, and is classified as a *main sequence* star. Depending on their size and mass, stars go through definite life cycles. Stars such as the sun start out as nebulas. They become red giants as they use up their hydrogen fuel, and they eventually end up as black dwarfs. More massive stars explode and end up as neutron stars or black holes.

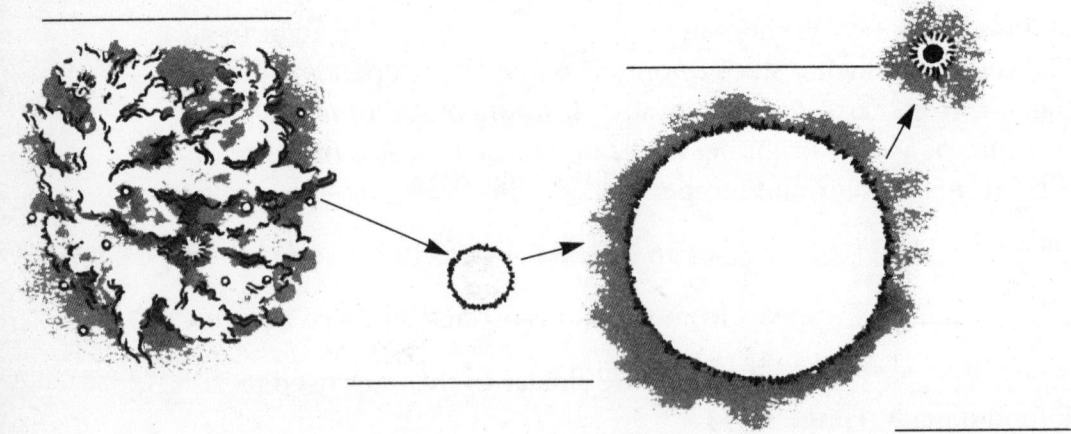

Name _____ Date _____

1. Many of the stars we can see are classified as _____ stars. **(page C88)**

2. A giant star may eventually explode into a _____. **(page C88)**

3. Describe the life cycle of a main sequence star like our sun. **(pages C88–C89)**

_____
_____
_____
_____
_____
_____

Review the Main Ideas

- Like all stars, the sun is a glowing globe of hot gas. And, like other stars, the sun is a source of tremendous energy.
- Stars release energy in a variety of forms. Light energy makes stars visible from Earth.
- Absolute magnitude can be used to classify stars. The sun, a star of average magnitude, is a main sequence star.

Check the Facts

Fill in the blanks.

Much of the energy on Earth comes from the _____, which is a main sequence _____ with an absolute _____ of +5. Most of the energy of the _____ is produced in its _____, where nuclear fission takes place. Most of the light of the _____, however, comes from the glowing gases of its _____. When a main sequence _____, like the _____, uses up all its fuel, it turns into a _____, then into a _____, and finally into a _____.

Section D • *Stars Near and Far*

Workbook
Unit C • StarBase Earth   C19

Name _____ Date _____

SECTION A WORKBOOK

Properties of Matter

Science Concept
Matter has properties that can be observed, described, and classified.

Vocabulary (pages D94–D95)

International System of Units	properties
mass	volume
matter	weight

Lesson 1 Summary (pages D13–D22)

As you read the summary, fill in the blanks with vocabulary terms from above. Then answer the questions that follow.

Everything we see, touch, taste, and smell is _____.
Matter is anything that has mass and takes up space. We can tell different substances, or objects of matter, apart by their characteristics,

or _____. Some of these properties are color, taste, and odor. Some properties of a substance always stay the same. For example, the color, taste, and smell of an orange are the same whether the orange is small or large, whole or sliced.

1. **Describe what matter is. (page D13)**

   _____
   _____

2. **Describe an orange according to its properties. (page D13)**

   _____
   _____
   _____

3. **Explain what properties of matter are described in "Do Me a Flavor." (pages D14–D18)**

   _____
   _____
   _____

Section A • Properties of Matter   Unit D • Cooking with Science

Name _____ Date _____

Lesson 2 Summary (pages D23–D31)

As you read the summary, fill in the blanks with vocabulary terms from page D1. Then answer the questions that follow.

Another way that matter can be described is by measurement. You use measurements in almost everything you do. When everyone agrees to use the same units of measurement, they are using *standard units*. Scientists from around the world have adopted the

_____, or *SI,* for a standard of measurement. People use these standard units to make all kinds of measurements every day. For example, cooking requires measuring

_____, or the amount of space something takes up. When you measure the amount of matter in an object, you are

measuring _____. People often confuse mass with

_____, which is a measure of the force of gravity pulling on an object. Weight varies with the gravitational force on an object, but mass remains the same.

1. Why do we measure using standard units instead of measuring with any kind of units? **(pages D23–D26)**

_____

_____

_____

_____

2. Complete the chart by filling in the symbol for the appropriate SI unit. **(pages D26–D30)**

	SI Unit	SI Symbol
Length	meter	
Mass	gram	
Volume of solids	cubic centimeter	
Temperature	degrees Celsius	

Name _____ Date _____

Lesson 3 Summary (pages D32–D35)

As you read the summary, fill in the blanks with the following terms: condensation, evaporation, phases, phase changes. *Then answer the questions that follow.*

Matter can also be found in solid, liquid, and gas states, or

_____. Some matter can go through all three

_____ as a result of heating or cooling. Water, for example, forms a solid at freezing temperatures, and when heated, melts into a liquid. As a liquid, water can change into a gas through

_____ and can once again, through cooling, become

a liquid by _____.

1. In the boxes below, show which is the solid, liquid, or gas by labeling each. **(pages D32–D35)**

_____   _____   _____

2. Explain why condensation forms on a glass containing a cold drink. **(page D33)**

_____
_____
_____

3. Explain how evaporation occurs. **(pages D32–D34)**

_____
_____
_____

Section A • Properties of Matter   Unit D • Cooking with Science   Workbook D3

Name _____ Date _____

Review the Main Ideas

- Matter is anything that has mass and takes up space.
- Different substances or objects of matter can be identified by their characteristics, or properties.
- Standard units are units of measurement that everyone agrees to use.
- The International System of Units, or SI, is a standard of measurement.
- Volume is the amount of space that something takes up.
- Mass is the measure of the amount of matter in an object.
- Weight is the measure of the force of gravity pulling on an object.
- Matter can be found in three states, or phases—solid, liquid, and gas.
- Condensation occurs when water vapor changes to a liquid.
- Evaporation occurs when a liquid changes to a gas.

Check the Vocabulary

Match the terms at the right with the definitions at the left.

____ 1. the amount of space an object takes up	a. propreties
____ 2. anything that has volume and mass. Gases, liquids, and solids are all examples.	b. International System of Units
____ 3. the measure of the force of gravity pulling on an object	c. volume
____ 4. the characteristics used to identify a substance. Color, taste, and odor are examples.	d. mass
____ 5. measure of the amount of matter in an object	e. matter
____ 6. the standard system of measurement used by scientists	f. weight

Name _____ Date _____

SECTION B WORKBOOK

Changes in Matter

Science Concept
Matter is made up of basic units. Matter can be combined, separated, mixed, and altered.

Vocabulary (pages D94–D95)

atom	element	physical change
chemical change	mixture	solution
colloid	molecule	suspension
compound		

Lesson 1 Summary (pages D37–D40)

As you read the summary, fill in the blanks with vocabulary terms from above.

The smallest building block of matter that retains the properties of matter is the _____. A single crystal of salt or grain of rice is made up of millions of atoms. Atoms are too small to be seen, except with very powerful microscopes.

An _____ is made up of only one kind of atom. Few of the things you see around you are pure elements. Wood, plastic, and steel are made of molecules that consist of many kinds of atoms.

A substance made of two or more elements chemically combined is called a _____. When two or more atoms combine, they form a _____. A molecule is the smallest particle of matter that consists of more than one atom.

Underline the best answer.

1. The smallest building block of matter is ... **(page D37)**
   a. a molecule.   b. an element.   c. an atom.   d. a compound.

2. ... is made up of only one kind of atom. **(page D40)**
   a. A molecule   b. An element   c. An atom   d. A compound

Name_____ Date_____

3. ... is a substance made of two or more elements chemically combined. **(page D40)**   a. A molecule   b. An element   c. An atom   d. A compound

4. When two or more atoms combine, they form ... **(page D40)**
   a. a molecule.   b. an element.   c. an atom.   d. a compound.

Lesson 2 Summary (pages D41–D48)

As you read the summary, fill in the blanks with vocabulary terms from page D5.

In a _____, the parts keep their properties, even though the parts are mixed together. A _____ is a mixture in which the composition is the same throughout. A _____ is a solution in which one of the parts is a liquid. Suspensions are very common in everyday life.

When you are making a gelatin dessert mold, you are making another type of mixture. The gelatin in the dessert is a mixture called a

_____. In a colloid, the particles do not dissolve, but they are so small that they do not settle out. They remain suspended because they are constantly moving.

Underline the best answer.

1. In ... the parts keep their own properties. **(page D42)**
   a. a suspension   b. a solution   c. a mixture   d. a colloid

2. ... are mixtures in which the composition is the same throughout. **(page D44)**
   a. Suspensions   b. Solutions   c. Mixtures   d. Colloids

3. ... is a mixture in which one of the parts is a liquid. **(page D45)**
   a. A suspension   b. A solution   c. A mixture   d. A colloid

4. ... is a mixture in which the particles do not settle out. **(page D46)**
   a. A suspension   b. A solution   c. A mixture   d. A colloid

5. Describe what the solvent and solute of a solution are. **(page D44)**

_____

_____

_____

_____

Name _____ Date _____

Lesson 3 Summary (pages D49–D61)

As you read the summary, fill in the blanks with vocabulary terms from page D5. Then answer the questions that follow.

A _____ results when two or more elements combine chemically. As a result, you end up with something you didn't have before. You have observed the formation of rust. Rust is a compound.

Rust results from the combining of atoms of the _____ oxygen in air with atoms of the element iron.

   Water is also a compound. Each molecule of the compound water is

made up of two atoms of hydrogen and one _____ of oxygen. Hydrogen and oxygen are gases, but when they combine as H_2O, they form the clear liquid water.

   Another example of a compound is salt. Salt is made up of the elements sodium and chlorine. As an element, sodium is a solid that is dangerous to handle because it can burst into flames. Chlorine is a poisonous gas. But when sodium and chlorine are combined chemically in the ratio of one to one, they form salt (NaCl), a white crystal that is safe to handle and eat.

1. Explain the difference between a mixture and a compound. **(page D51)**

   _____

   _____

2. Explain how the compound water is formed. **(page D51)**

   _____

   _____

   _____

Name _____ Date _____

Lesson 4 Summary (pages D62–D65)

As you read the summary, fill in the blanks with vocabulary terms from page D5. Then answer the questions that follow.

There are two ways matter can change—chemically and physically. When elements combine to form a compound, a chemical change occurs. In a _____, a new chemical is formed from another type of matter. Burning charcoal is an example of a chemical change.

A _____ in matter is a change in matter that does not form a new chemical. Examples of physical changes are boiling, dissolving, evaporating, and freezing.

1. Explain the difference between a chemical change and a physical change. **(page D62)**

   _____

   _____

   _____

2. List some clues that a chemical change has occurred. **(page D62)**

   _____

   _____

   _____

3. Identify each example as a chemical change or a physical change. **(page D62)**

Example	Type of Change
balled-up piece of paper	
burned piece of paper	

Name _____ Date _____

Review the Main Ideas

- Atoms are the smallest building blocks of matter that still retain the properties of matter.
- Elements are made up of only one kind of atom.
- Compounds are substances made of two or more elements chemically combined.
- Molecules are combinations of two or more atoms.
- Mixtures are matter containing two or more substances that are not chemically combined.
- A solution is a mixture that includes a solvent and a solute.
- A suspension is a mixture in which solid particles can separate slowly from a gas or a liquid.
- A colloid is a mixture in which the very small particles do not separate but remain suspended.
- A chemical change is a change in which a new chemical forms from another type of matter.
- A physical change is a change in matter that does not form a new chemical.

Name_____ Date_____

Check the Vocabulary

Match the terms at the right with the definitions at the left.

____	1. two or more elements that have combined chemically and can be separated only by chemical changes	a. atom
____	2. matter containing two or more substances that are not chemically combined	b. element
____	3. a mixture that includes a solvent and a solute, the substance that is dissolved in the solvent	c. compound
____	4. the smallest building block of matter that retains the properties of matter	d. molecule
____	5. the smallest particle of matter that consists of more than one atom	e. mixture
____	6. a change in matter that does not form a new chemical	f. solution
____	7. a mixture in which the very small particles do not separate but remain suspended	g. suspension
____	8. a mixture in which solid particles can separate slowly from a gas or a liquid	h. colloid
____	9. a change in which a new chemical forms from another type of matter	i. chemical change
____	10. matter made up of only one kind of atom	j. physical change

Name _____ Date _____

SECTION C WORKBOOK

Heat

Science Concept
Heat is the transfer of thermal energy. It can be measured as the total kinetic energy of the motion of the atoms or molecules in a substance.

Vocabulary (pages D94–D95)

| heat | temperature |

Lesson 1 Summary (pages D67–D76)

As you read the summary, fill in the blanks with vocabulary terms from above. Then answer the questions that follow.

We know that all matter is made of tiny particles called molecules. These particles are in constant motion. Scientists know that

_____ is a form of energy. As an object becomes hotter, its atoms and molecules move faster. You can determine how hot

something is by taking its _____. Temperature is the measure of the average kinetic energy, or energy of movement, of the atoms and molecules in a substance or an object.

1. How is heat related to temperature? **(page D71)**

_____

_____

_____

2. What happens to solids, liquids, and gases when they are heated? **(pages D72–D73)**

_____

_____

_____

3. Label the appropriate molecule models as solid, liquid, or gas. **(page D70)**

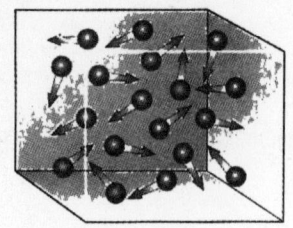 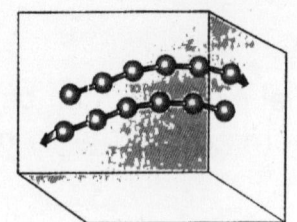 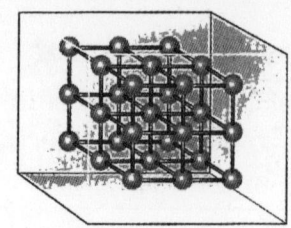

_____ _____ _____

Lesson 2 Summary (pages D77–D89)

As you read the summary, fill in the blanks with the following terms: conduction, convection, radiation. *Then answer the questions that follow.*

_____ is the movement of heat that occurs when atoms or molecules bump into one another. Through contact, kinetic energy, in the form of heat, is transferred.

_____ is the transfer of heat by currents of molecules in liquids and gases. As water near a heat source becomes hotter, its molecules begin moving faster and spreading out. The warmer water is less dense than the cooler water, so the warmer water is pushed up by the cooler, more dense water. This produces currents of warm water that carry heat.

In conduction and convection, the movement of molecules transfers heat. The sun's heat does not require the movement of molecules.

Instead, the heat is transferred by _____, or by infrared rays. Infrared rays are like light rays, but they cannot be seen. These rays travel in straight lines as fast as light. The sun's rays travel through space to Earth and produce radiant heat.

1. Explain how heat movement by conduction occurs. **(page D78)**

_____

_____

_____

_____

Name _____ Date _____

2. Explain how heat movement by convection occurs. **(page D80)**

_____

_____

_____

_____

3. Explain why heat energy from the sun reaches the Earth only by radiation. **(page D82)**

_____

_____

_____

_____

Review the Main Ideas

- Matter is made up of molecules that are in constant motion.
- Heat is a form of energy.
- Temperature is the measure of the average kinetic energy, or energy of movement, of the atoms and molecules in a substance or an object.
- Conduction is the movement of heat that occurs when atoms or molecules bump into one another.
- Convection is the transfer of heat by currents of molecules in liquids and gases.
- Radiation is the transfer of heat energy by infrared rays from the sun.

Check the Facts

Underline the best answer.

1. . . . is a form of energy that is produced by the movement of molecules in a substance.
   a. Temperature **b.** Conduction **c.** Heat **d.** Radiation

2. . . . is the measure of the average kinetic energy of the molecules in a substance or an object.
   a. Temperature **b.** Conduction **c.** Heat **d.** Radiation

Name _____ Date _____

Life on the Prairie

SECTION A WORKBOOK

Science Concept
Living things interact with each other and with their physical environments.

Vocabulary (pages E94–E95)

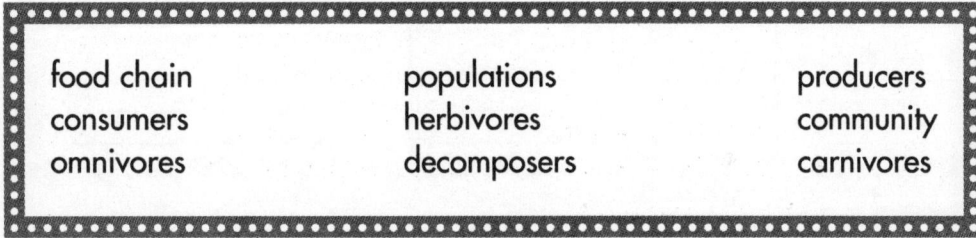

food chain	populations	producers
consumers	herbivores	community
omnivores	decomposers	carnivores

Lesson 1 Summary (pages E13–E18)

Read the summary, and then answer the questions that follow.

Prairies are open, grassy lands that are found in many parts of the world. Prairies are large land areas that are flat or have gently rolling hills. Sometimes this grassy land is used for farming and grazing, but people have also built large cities on the prairies.

Prairies can have different plants, depending on where the prairie is found and the amount of rainfall it receives. *Tallgrass prairies,* where the grasses and flowers grow very high, receive more rain than other prairies. *Mixed-grass prairies* have a mixture of tall and short grasses that grow in clumps like small islands. *Short-grass prairies* receive little rain. Often, cacti and sagebrush are found among the grasses of short-grass prairies.

1. In the boxes below, draw and identify each kind of prairie. **(pages E13–E14)**

short-grass prairie	**mixed-grass prairie**	**tallgrass prairie**

Section A • Life on the Prairie

Workbook
Unit E • Prairie Dog Tales   **E1**

Name _____ Date _____

2. Match the grass with the prairie it is found on. **(pages E15–E17)**

   Junegrass   buffalo grass   wild rye
   big bluestem grass blue gamma   cordgrass
   green needlegrass little bluestem grass   sagebrush

Short-grass prairie	Mixed-grass prairie	Tallgrass prairie
_____	_____	_____
_____	_____	_____
_____	_____	_____

3. What is the difference between short-grass, mixed-grass, and tallgrass prairies? **(pages E15–E17)**

   _____
   _____
   _____
   _____

Lesson 2 Summary (pages E19–E22)

Read the summary, and then answer the questions that follow.

There are many kinds of animals on the prairies. Some animals, such as bison, prairie dogs, and coyotes, are easy to see. To find other animals, you have to look closely at the earth, the flowers, and the grasses.

1. Name four animals found on the prairie. **(pages E19–E22)**

   _____   _____

   _____   _____

2. Why do Mark Hoogland and his father trap prairie dogs? **(pages E19–E22)**

   _____
   _____
   _____

Name _____ Date _____

Lesson 3 Summary (pages E23–E29)

As you read the summary, fill in the blanks with vocabulary terms from page E1. Then answer the questions that follow.

Each kind of plant and animal on the prairie has a "job." Plants are

_____. They get energy from the sun and use it to make

food from nutrients in the soil and air. Animals are _____.
They can't use energy from the sun directly, so they must get energy
from other living things. Some animals, such as bison, prairie dogs, and

squirrels, are _____. They get their energy from plants.
Eventually, some herbivores become food for other animals called

_____. Carnivores, such as badgers, coyotes, and hawks,
are meat-eaters. Some animals, such as bears and raccoons, are

_____. Omnivores eat both plants and animals.

The energy in the chain continues as scavengers consume the dead
animals on a prairie. Finally, insects, fungi, and bacteria, which are

_____, break dead animals into small parts that become
part of the soil. So, energy from the sun flows to plants, then to
herbivores, next to carnivores and omnivores, then to scavengers, and

finally to decomposers. We call this path the _____.

A prairie _____, like other environments, is

composed of all the plant and animal _____ that
are found in it. If conditions on the prairie change permanently,
the populations can change, and plants and animals may have
difficulty surviving.

Name _____ Date _____

1. Label each organism as an *herbivore*, a *carnivore*, an *omnivore*, a *decomposer*, or a *scavenger*.

_____ _____ _____

_____ _____

2. How are consumers different from producers? **(pages E24–E25)**

_____
_____
_____
_____

3. Fill in the missing boxes in the food chain. **(page E27)**

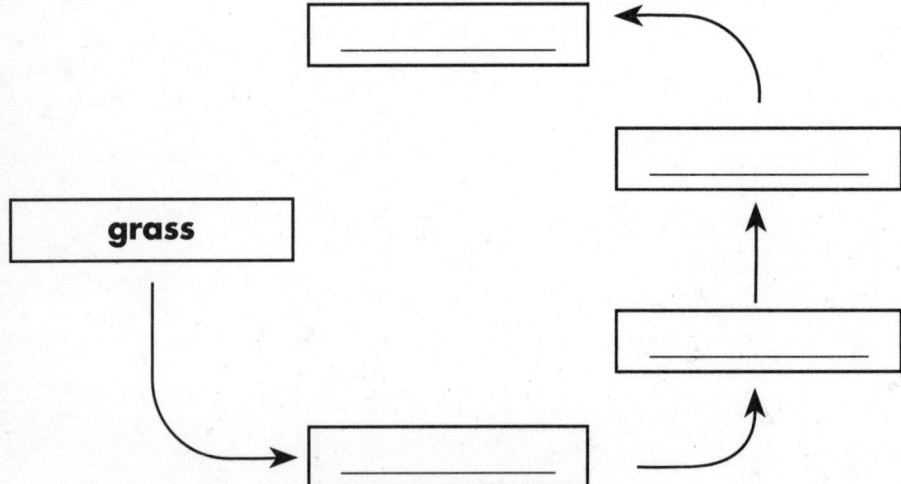

Workbook
E4 Unit E • Prairie Dog Tales   Section A • Life on the Prairie

Name _____ Date _____

4. How would the population of animals in a prairie community be affected if one animal is overhunted? (pages E28–E29)

_____

_____

_____

_____

- A grassy area that is flat or has gently rolling hills is called a prairie.
- There are tallgrass, mixed-grass, and short-grass prairies.
- Plants and animals all have a place on the prairie. Plants are producers, and animals are consumers.
- Animals that get their energy from plants are herbivores.
- Animals that are meat-eaters are carnivores.
- Animals that eat both plants and animals are omnivores.
- Scavengers consume dead animals on the prairie.
- Decomposers break the dead animals into small parts that become part of the soil.
- In the food chain, energy flows from the sun to herbivores, carnivores, omnivores, scavengers, and decomposers.
- If conditions on the prairie change permanently, plants and animals may not be able to survive.

Name _____ Date _____

Check the Vocabulary

Match the terms at the right with the definitions at the left.

____ 1. all the plants or animals of one kind that live in an area, such as all the prairie dogs living on a prairie	a. food chain
____ 2. a meat-eating animal	b. consumers
____ 3. the path of producers and consumers along which energy passes through a community	c. omnivore
____ 4. organisms, such as grasses, that make their own food	d. population
____ 5. organisms that get energy by eating other living things	e. herbivore
____ 6. groups of plants and animals that live in the same environment	f. decomposer
____ 7. an animal that eats plants and animals	g. producers
____ 8. a plant-eating animal	h. communities
____ 9. any living organism that breaks down dead plants and animals into nutrients that can be used by other living organisms	i. carnivore

Workbook
E6   Unit E • Prairie Dog Tales   Section A • Life on the Prairie

Name _____ Date _____

Cycles and Soils

SECTION B WORKBOOK

Science Concept
Soils contain nutrients that are cycled throughout the environment.

Lesson 1 Summary (pages E31–E34)

Read the summary, and then answer the questions that follow.

In a prairie community, plants and animals interact with the physical environment—the water, the air, and the soil. The amount of rainfall that a prairie receives determines what kinds of plants can grow there, and the plant life, in turn, determines the kinds of herbivores and carnivores that are found there.

Water is essential to a prairie. When it rains, plants use the water that they need, and then the excess water forms pools or soaks into the ground. Water is constantly being recycled on the prairie. The sun evaporates the water, and then water vapor condenses, forming clouds. The droplets grow larger and fall as rain or snow, starting the cycle all over.

1. Label the parts of the water cycle. **(page E33)**

Name _____ Date _____

2. What do plants release into the air? **(pages E32–E34)**
   _____
   _____

3. Explain how carnivores are part of the oxygen-carbon cycle. **(pages E32–E34)**
   _____
   _____
   _____
   _____

4. Draw and label an example of the oxygen-carbon cycle. **(page E34)**

   [   ]
   [   ]
   [   ]
   [   ]
   [   ]
   [   ]

5. Why is it important that we take care of the water supply on the prairie? **(pages E32–E34)**
   _____
   _____
   _____

Name _____ Date _____

Lesson 2 Summary (pages E35–E41)

Read the summary, and then answer the questions that follow.

The plant and animal life that exists on the prairie also depends on soil. Soil is formed from *parent material,* or rock that is on or near the Earth's surface. Wind and water break down the parent material into small pieces in a process called *weathering.* Plants begin to grow in the rock pieces. Insects move in. As the plants and animals die, they break down in the soil and make it richer.

Soil can wear away faster than it forms. Soil that took thousands of years to form can be carried away in an afternoon by wind or water. There are many ways to prevent soil from wearing away, or *eroding.* Plants that cover soil can keep the wind from blowing the soil away. Farmers can plant their crops across hills rather than up and down them to help keep the soil in place. This is called *contour farming.*

1. Label each layer of the soil. **(pages E38–E39)**

_____

_____

_____

2. Describe how soil is formed. **(pages E37–E39)**

_____
_____
_____
_____
_____

3. Why do farmers plant cover crops? **(page E41)**

_____
_____

Name_____ Date_____

4. What are two different things that farmers can do to keep their soil from wearing away? **(page E41)**

_____

_____

Review the Main Ideas

- Plants and animals of the prairie interact with the water and soil.
- The amount of rainfall determines the types of plants that will grow on a prairie.
- Water is reused and recycled over and over again in the water cycle.
- The plant and animal life on the prairie depends on the soil.
- Soil is formed from parent material.
- Soil can erode, or wear away, faster than it forms.
- Farmers can plant cover crops and do contour farming to keep the soil from eroding.

Name _____ Date _____

Check the Facts

Answer the following questions.

1. Match the terms at the right with the definitions at the left.

____ 1. process that breaks down parent material	a. inorganic
____ 2. not from living organisms	b. organic material
____ 3. hardy plants that grow in rock pieces	c. parent material
____ 4. original rock from which soil is formed	d. weathering
____ 5. remains of once-living organisms	e. pioneers

2. How long does it take for 1 centimeter of soil to form?

_____

3. Does soil form more quickly in warm climates or cold?

_____

4. What are two things that can cause soil to erode?

_____   _____

Section B • Cycles and Soils

Name _____ Date _____

SECTION C WORKBOOK

World Biomes

Science Concept
Communities around the world are both similar and different.

Vocabulary (pages E94–E95)

```
biome
```

Lesson 1 Summary (pages E43–E49)

Read the summary, and then answer the questions that follow.

Prairie-like communities are found in many parts of the world. In South America, prairies are referred to as *pampas*. In Asia they are called *steppes*. They may have different plants and animals, but they all have a similar climate. Prairies in all parts of the world are part of the *grasslands biome*.

1. Match the grassland community to the continent. **(pages E44–E47)**

Continent	Grassland
__b__ Asia	a. prairies
__c__ South America	b. steppes
__a__ North America	c. pampas

*Use the precipitation and temperature chart on **pages E48–E49** to answer the following questions.*

2. Which grassland has the coldest average temperature in January?

   _____

3. What is the total average precipitation the North American prairie receives in one year? _____

Workbook
E12 Unit E • Prairie Dog Tales   Section C • World Biomes

Name _____ Date _____

4. How are the South American pampas different from the Asian steppes? How are they similar? **(pages E44–E47)**

_____

_____

_____

Lesson 2 Summary (pages E50–E65)

Read the summary, and then answer the questions that follow.

A *biome* is a large community of plants and animals. The type of biome is determined by climate and the kinds of plants found there. There are six major land biomes in the world.

Tropical rain forests grow where the climate is warm and rainy. Most of the animal life is found in the trees. Rain forests are important because they produce oxygen, which supports life.

Deciduous forests have warm or hot summers and cold winters. Deciduous trees lose their leaves every fall. Deer, squirrels, foxes, owls, and snakes are found in deciduous forests.

Boreal forests grow in places with very cold, snowy winters and short growing seasons. The trees are mostly evergreens. In this type of forest you will find deer, bears, snowshoe hares, and beavers.

On the *arctic tundra,* the winters are long and cold and the summers are short and cool. Animals on the tundra, such as the snowy owl, are adapted for cold weather. They also blend in with the snow.

Grasslands have winters that are cold and snowy and summers that are hot and dry. Many small animals, such as ground squirrels, prairie dogs, and many kinds of birds, are found in the grasslands.

Because *deserts* receive very little rainfall, the plants there are far apart so they don't compete with each other for moisture. The desert supports many animals, such as mice, snakes, and coyotes.

Name _____ Date _____

1. Use the boldface words from the summary to complete the table.

Biome	Description
_____	long, cold winters; animals blend with snow
_____	warm summers, cold winters; trees lose leaves
_____	receive little rainfall; plants are far apart
_____	cold, snowy winters; evergreen trees
_____	hot, dry summers; home to prairie dogs
_____	warm and rainy; produces much oxygen

2. Identify the biome each animal lives in.

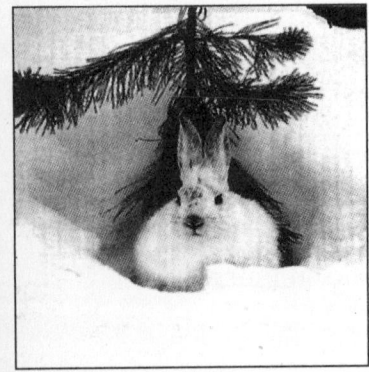  

_____   _____   _____

_____   _____   _____

Name _____ Date _____

5. Identify and label each biome on the world map.

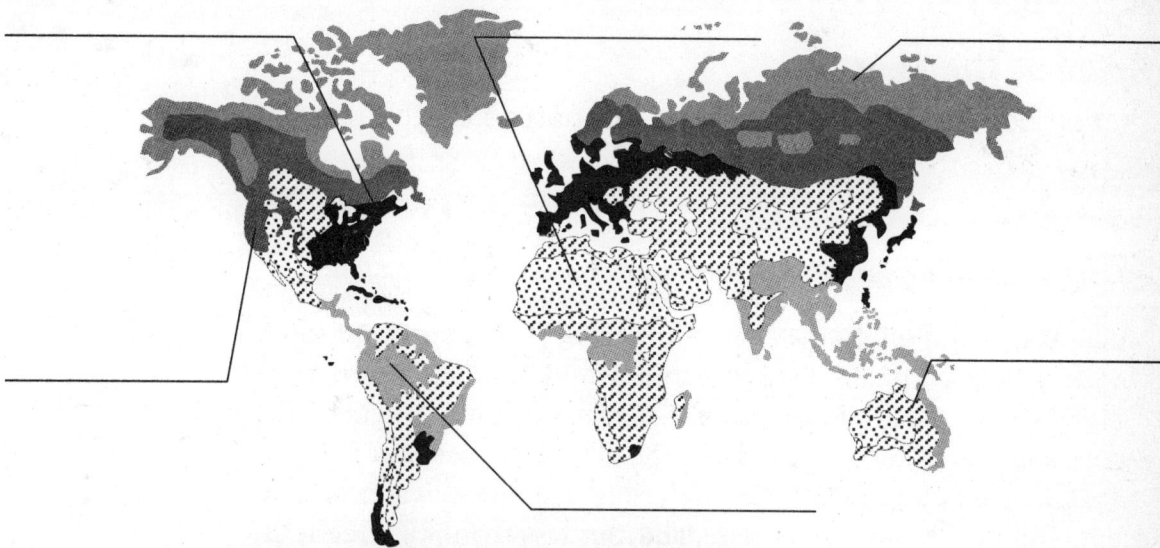

- Prairie-like communities are found in many parts of the world. In South America, prairies are called pampas. In Asia, prairies are called steppes.
- Prairies are part of the grasslands biome.
- Biomes are large communities determined by climate.
- There are six major land biomes: tropical rain forests, deciduous forests, boreal forests, arctic tundra, grasslands, and deserts.

Answer the following questions.

1. A biome is _____
   _____.

2. Name the biome where you live. _____

3. Describe the climate of the arctic tundra.
   _____
   _____
   _____

Name_____ Date_____

People and the Prairie

Science Concept

Human activities affect the balance of nature on the prairie.

Lesson 1 Summary (pages E67–E71)

Read the summary, and then answer the questions that follow.

Much of the land on prairies has been changed by people for their use. People have used prairie land for farming and building. When people use grasslands, the biome changes. If the land is not used carefully, the plants, animals, water, soil, and even the air can be destroyed.

People need certain things to live. They need food, water, and shelter. All of these things require land, but less than 30 percent of Earth's surface is land. Of that 30 percent, only 13 percent is land usable for farming.

1. Fill in the blanks with the percentage. **(page E70)**

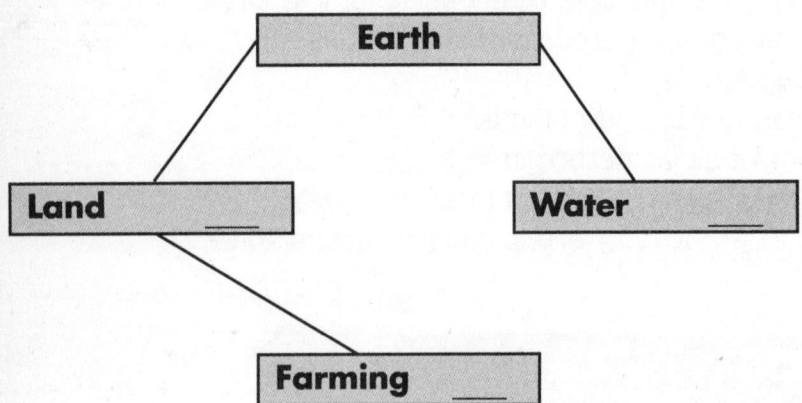

2. Name two ways that people change the prairies. **(pages E68–E69)**

   _____   _____

3. Look at the circle graphs found on **page E70**. What continent has the largest percent of land suitable for farming?

   _____

4. What happens to life on the prairie if the population of a natural predator is killed off? **(page E71)**

   _____

   _____

Name _____ Date _____

5. Complete the following chart. (page E70)

Land Area	Agricultural Land	Grazing Land
North and Central America	___%	___%
South America	___%	___%
Eurasia	___%	___%
Africa	___%	___%
Australia	___%	___%

Lesson 2 Summary (pages E72–E83)

Read the summary, and then answer the questions that follow.

People change the land when they use it. Farming, grazing, and building all change the natural prairie. As people use land, they also produce wastes. Wastes can be harmless or they can destroy the environment. Some farmers use chemical fertilizers and pesticides that can harm the soil and the water supply. Some kinds of pollution, such as landfills, are very visible. Other kinds, such as chemicals in the air, are harder to see.

One way for people to help control pollution is to *recycle*. Aluminum cans, plastic, and newspaper are just a few things that can be recycled. Another way is for farmers to use alternatives to pesticides, such as natural predators, to get rid of pests.

1. Name four ways that people pollute the prairie. (pages E75–E77)

_____   _____

_____   _____

2. Name three ways in which people can control pollution. (page E80)

a. _____

b. _____

c. _____

Name_____ Date_____

3. Look at the illustration of the prairie. List all the ways that people have changed the land.

_____   _____
_____   _____
_____   _____
_____   _____
_____   _____

4. Why is it important to recycle? **(page E80)**

_____
_____

Name _____ Date _____

Lesson 3 Summary (pages E84–E89)

Read the summary, and then answer the questions that follow.

People can change and damage the prairie in a short amount of time. Once land has been harmed, it is difficult or impossible to undo all the harmful effects. Sometimes, small areas can be restored to their original conditions. Various groups of people are working to restore prairies to their natural condition.

1. What is the process called in which a pond changes into a meadow?

   (pages E84–E85) _____

2. Why is it important to restore prairie land? **(pages E86–E89)**

   _____
   _____
   _____
   _____

- Prairie land has been changed by people.
- People need land to live, but only a small portion of land is usable for farming.
- Farming, grazing, and building all change the land.
- People can damage the prairie by polluting it.
- People can save prairie land by making changes in the way they use the land and by restoring the land.

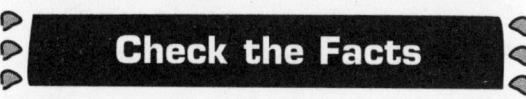

Answer the following question.

What is a conservationist?

_____
_____
_____

Name _____ Date _____

SECTION A WORKBOOK

How Does It Move?

Science Concept
The motion of objects can be described and classified.

Vocabulary (pages F94–F96)

frame of reference	acceleration
velocity	energy

Lesson 1 Summary (pages F13–F15)

Read the summary, and then answer the questions that follow.

The physical world is constantly in motion. Each time you describe something that is moving, you are comparing it with another object or a background that you assume is not moving. This background or object is your *frame of reference*. The most basic frame of reference we use is the movement of the Earth around the sun. Even ancient people observed the Earth's relationship to the sun and the stars. They built structures, such as Casa Grande, in Arizona, to observe the apparent movement of the sun and the stars.

1. Comparing the motion of an object with a background that is not moving is using a _____. **(page F14)**

2. When you change your frame of reference, your perception of _____ changes, too. **(page F14)**

3. Give an example of a frame of reference you have experienced. **(pages F13–F14)**

_____
_____
_____
_____
_____

Section A • How Does It Move?
Workbook
Unit F • Amusement Park   F1

Name _____ Date _____

Lesson 2 Summary (pages F16–F19)

Read the summary, and then answer the questions that follow.

The motion of objects can be measured. Speed is the distance an object moves in a given unit of time. But speed does not tell us everything about an object's motion. *Velocity* is the speed of an object in a certain direction. When the direction of an object changes, its velocity changes. If the speed of an object changes, its velocity changes.

1. A roller coaster climbs a hill at 8 kilometers per hour. Its velocity is _____ kilometers per hour _____. **(page F19)**

2. While the roller coaster makes a sharp turn, its speed remains the same, but its _____ changes as its direction changes. **(page F19)**

3. On a length of flat track, the roller coaster's speed is 30 kilometers per hour, and its velocity is _____ kilometers per hour _____. **(page F19)**

4. As the roller coaster travels down a hill at a speed of 50 kilometers per hour, its velocity is _____ kilometers per hour _____. **(page F19)**

5. How are speed and velocity related? **(page F19)**

_____

_____

Lesson 3 Summary (pages F20–F23)

Read the summary, and then answer the questions that follow.

The rate of change in velocity, or the change in velocity over time, is called *acceleration*. Whether an object is speeding up, slowing down, or changing direction, it is accelerating. When an object slows down, or the velocity decreases, we sometimes say the object is decelerating. However, in scientific language, any change in velocity is called acceleration.

Name _____ Date _____

1. A cyclist is traveling along a straight road at a constant speed. The cyclist coasts as she enters a wide curve. Coming out of the curve, she starts to speed down a gentle hill. She then slows down as she starts to climb a steep hill. Identify all examples of acceleration in this story. **(pages F22–F23)**

_____

_____

_____

2. How are velocity and acceleration related? **(page F22)**

_____

_____

Lesson 4 Summary (pages F24–F31)

Read the summary, and then answer the questions that follow.

Motion involves energy. *Energy* is the ability to cause change. At the top of a hill, a roller coaster has *potential energy*—the energy stored in an object. As the roller coaster descends, its potential energy is converted to *kinetic energy,* the energy of movement. The energy stored in an object that can bend or stretch and then return to its original shape is called *elastic potential energy.* This energy can be observed in items such as a rubber band or a stretched spring. The energy an object has because of its ability to fall is *gravitational potential energy.* A marble held above the floor has this kind of potential energy. When you drop the marble, the gravitational potential energy is converted into kinetic energy. The higher you hold the marble, the greater the energy it has.

An object in motion has *momentum*. An object's momentum is its mass multiplied by its velocity. If its mass or velocity is large, an object will have a large momentum. The more momentum an object has, the harder it is to stop the object or to change its direction.

Underline the best answer.

1. A diver poised on a diving board has . . .   **a.** kinetic energy.
   b. mechanical energy.   **c.** gravitational potential energy.
   d. elastic potential energy. **(page F28)**

Name_____ Date_____

2. As the diver jumps, the board bends down. At this point the board has ... **a.** kinetic energy. **b.** mechanical energy. **c.** gravitational potential energy. **d.** elastic potential energy. **(page F26)**

3. As the diver plunges into the water, the diver has ... **a.** kinetic energy. **b.** mechanical energy. **c.** gravitational potential energy. **d.** elastic potential energy. **(page F24)**

4. Which has the greatest momentum? **a.** a bowling ball traveling at 10 kph **b.** a bowling ball traveling at 20 kph **c.** a basketball traveling at 10 kph **d.** a basketball traveling at 20 kph **(page F31)**

5. Describe the changes in energy that take place when children hit a piñata, the piñata breaks, and the candy and toys fall out. **(page F28)**

_____
_____
_____
_____

Review the Main Ideas

- When you compare an object that is moving with a background you assume is not moving, the background is your frame of reference.
- The motion of objects can be measured. Speed is the distance an object moves in a given unit of time.
- Velocity is the speed of an object in a certain direction.
- When the speed or direction of an object changes, its velocity changes.
- The change in velocity over time is called acceleration.
- Whether an object is speeding up, slowing down, or changing direction, it is accelerating.
- Energy is the ability to cause change.
- Potential energy is the energy stored in an object, sometimes due to its position.
- Kinetic energy is the energy of movement.
- The energy stored in an object that can bend or stretch and then return to its original shape is called elastic potential energy.

Name _____ Date _____

- The energy an object has because of its ability to fall is gravitational potential energy.
- An object in motion has momentum, which is its mass multiplied by its velocity.

Check the Facts

Fill in the blanks with the correct terms.

1. The ability to cause change is called _____.

2. _____ energy is the energy of movement.

3. Stored energy is called _____ energy.

4. The rate of change in velocity of an object is called _____.

5. The speed of an object in a certain direction is _____.

6. Comparing the motion of an object with a background that you assume is not moving is using a _____.

Section A • How Does It Move?

Workbook
Unit F • Amusement Park F5

Name _____ Date _____

Pushes and Pulls

SECTION B WORKBOOK

Science Concept
Forces have magnitude and direction.

Vocabulary (pages F94–F96)

```
force                mass
gravity              weight
```

Lesson 1 Summary (pages F33–F36)

As you read the summary, fill in the blank with a vocabulary term from above. Then answer the questions that follow.

A _____ is a push or a pull. A force can start an object moving, change the direction and rate of its motion, or change the shape of the object. Any force acts in a specific direction with a specific size or strength. Forces can be combined to increase their effect. You can illustrate a force by using an arrow. The head of the arrow shows the direction of the force. The tail of the arrow identifies the point where the force is exerted. The length or thickness of the arrow represents the size, or strength, of the force.

1. In the diagrams below, draw arrows to indicate the direction and strength of the forces. **(page F35)**

Name _____ Date _____

2. Identify the following activities as pushes or pulls. Write *push* or *pull* on the line in front of the statement. **(page F35)**

_____ hitting a tennis ball   _____ painting a wall

_____ brushing your teeth   _____ brushing your hair

_____ writing with a pencil   _____ rowing a boat

_____ pedaling a bicycle   _____ climbing a rope

Lesson 2 Summary (pages F37–F40)

As you read the summary, fill in the blanks with vocabulary terms from page F6. Then answer the question that follows.

_____ is the force that pulls all objects in the universe toward one another. Earth is surrounded by a gravitational field that decreases in strength as the distance from Earth increases. The size of the force of gravity between any two objects is determined by the masses of the objects and the distance between them.

_____ is the amount of matter in an object.

If you dropped a baseball, a golf ball, and a tennis ball from the same height at the same time, which ball would hit the ground first? Explain. **(page F38)**

_____
_____
_____
_____
_____
_____
_____
_____

Section B • Pushes and Pulls

Workbook
Unit F • Amusement Park   F7

Name _____ Date _____

Lesson 3 Summary (pages F41–F45)

As you read the summary, fill in the blank with a vocabulary term from page F6. Then answer the questions that follow.

Every object has a center of mass, or center of gravity—the point at which gravity seems to act. _____ is the force of gravity pulling an object toward the center of another object. So, on Earth, the weight of an object is the force of gravity acting on that object. The moon has less mass than the Earth and so attracts with less force. Although your amount of matter, or mass, would not change, you would weigh less on the moon.

Forces can be measured. The unit used to measure force is the newton (N). One newton is equal to the force of gravity exerted by the Earth on a 100-g mass. So, a newton is approximately equal to the weight of a 100-g mass. Newtons can also be used to measure the amount of force you need to move something a certain distance, as when you stretch an elastic cord.

1. Denver, Colorado, has an altitude of about 17,500 meters (5,280 feet). New Orleans, Louisiana, is about 3 meters (9.9 feet) below sea level. In which city would you weigh more? Explain. **(page F41)**

_____
_____
_____
_____
_____

2. Describe the difference between mass and weight. **(pages F38, F41)**

_____
_____
_____
_____
_____
_____

Name _____ Date _____

Review the Main Ideas

- A force is a push or a pull. A force can start an object moving, change the direction and rate of its motion, or change the shape of the object.
- Any force acts in a specific direction with a specific size or strength.
- Gravity is the force that pulls all objects in the universe toward one another.
- The size of the force of gravity between two objects is determined by their masses and the distance between the objects.
- Mass is the amount of matter in an object.
- Weight is the force of gravity pulling an object toward the center of another object.
- The unit used to measure force is the newton. One newton is equal to the force of gravity exerted by the Earth on a 100-g mass.

Check the Facts

Fill in the blanks with the correct terms or phrases.

1. A force is either a _____ or a _____.

2. A force can start an object _____, change the _____ and _____ of its motion, or change the _____ of the object.

3. Any force acts in a specific _____ with a specific _____ or strength.

4. _____ is the force that pulls all objects in the universe toward one another.

5. Earth is surrounded by a _____.

6. The strength of Earth's gravitational field _____ as the distance from Earth _____.

Section B • Pushes and Pulls

Workbook
Unit F • Amusement Park   F9

Name_____ Date_____

7. The strength of the Earth's gravitational field is described by an object's _____ toward Earth's center.

8. The size of the force of gravity between any two objects is determined by their masses and by the _____ between the objects.

9. _____ is the amount of matter in an object.

10. Two objects having different masses, falling together, will land _____.

Name _____ Date _____

The Forces Are with You

SECTION C WORKBOOK

Science Concept
Forces cause a change in the motion of objects.

Vocabulary (pages F94–F96)

| friction | inertia |

Lesson 1 Summary (pages F47–F49)

Read the summary, and then answer the questions that follow.

Forces can affect the motion of objects. Gravity is a force that acts on all objects in the universe. Gravity can affect the motion of a baseball that is thrown. Gravity causes an object to change direction as it falls.

Circular motion, such as a swinging ride at an amusement park, can be affected by the force of cables holding the cars. The collision of objects can affect motion also. A collision can start motion, stop motion, change the speed of motion, or change the direction of motion.

Look at the diagrams below, and then complete each diagram according to the directions given. Then describe the force that is affecting the motion in each case. (pages F47–F49)

1.
2.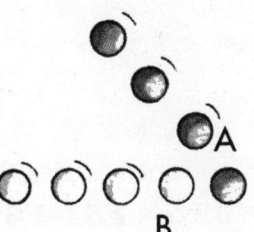
3.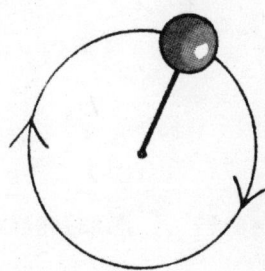

Diagram the path of the ball as it rolls off the table.

Draw the path of each ball after the two collide.

Show the path of the ball as the string is cut.

Section C • The Forces Are with You

Name_____ Date_____

Lesson 2 Summary (pages F50–F53)

Read the summary, and then follow the directions below.

Some forces result in movement, and some do not. Two forces that are equal in size but opposite in direction are *balanced forces*. Balanced forces do not change the position of an object. If you and your friend each push on opposite sides of a swinging door with the same amount of force, the door will not move. To cause a change in motion, forces must be unbalanced. *Unbalanced forces* are opposite and unequal. Suppose two teams of students of approximately the same size and strength play tug of war. Team 1 has two members, and Team 2 has four members. It is likely that Team 1 will be pulled across the center line, because the forces of the teams are unbalanced.

In the space below, draw and label with lines of force an example of balanced forces and an example of unbalanced forces. Use examples other than those described in the paragraph above. **(pages F50–F53)**

Lesson 3 Summary (pages F54–F60)

Read the summary, and then complete the activity that follows.

Friction is the force that resists motion between the surfaces of two objects that are touching. When objects slide over one another, the friction that results is called *sliding friction*. The friction produced by round objects such as wheels or balls is called *rolling friction*.

Fluid friction is the force exerted by a fluid (a liquid or a gas) on an object moving through the fluid. The direction of the force is the opposite of the direction in which the object is moving.

Workbook
F12 Unit F • Amusement Park   Section C • The Forces Are with You

Name _____ Date _____

Below each picture, write the type of friction most likely at work in each situation. **(pages F55–F59)**

_____

_____

_____

_____

_____

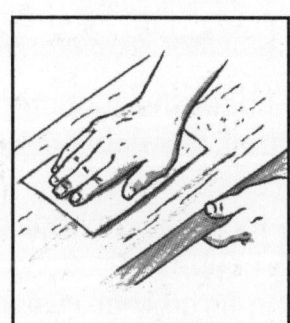

_____

Lesson 4 Summary (pages F61–F69)

Read the summary, and then complete the concept map that follows.

Motion and forces were described by Sir Isaac Newton in the seventeenth century. Newton's first law of motion states that objects at rest tend to stay at rest and that objects that are moving tend to continue moving. This resistance to changes in motion is called *inertia*.

Newton's second law of motion states that when an unbalanced force is applied to an object, the object accelerates. The amount of acceleration depends on the mass of the object and the amount of force applied to it. Newton's third law of motion states that for every force there is an equal and opposite force. These forces are called *action* and *reaction* forces.

Section C • The Forces Are with You

Name _____ Date _____

Review the Main Ideas

- Forces can affect the motion of objects.
- Two forces that are equal in size but opposite in direction are balanced forces.
- Unbalanced forces are opposite and unequal.
- To cause a change in motion, forces must be unbalanced.
- Friction is the force that resists motion between two touching surfaces.
- Newton's first law of motion states that objects at rest tend to stay at rest and that objects that are moving tend to continue moving.
- The resistance to change in motion is called inertia.
- Newton's second law states that when an unbalanced force is applied to an object, the object accelerates.
- Newton's third law states that for every force, there is an equal and opposite force.

Name _____ Date _____

Check the Facts

Match the terms at the right with the description at the left.

____	1. force exerted on a parachute	a. Newton's first law of motion
____	2. two forces equal in size but opposite in direction	b. sliding friction
____	3. inertia	c. unbalanced forces
____	4. force exerted by a liquid or a gas on an object moving through the liquid or gas	d. air resistance
____	5. force that resists motion between two touching surfaces	e. Newton's second law of motion
____	6. For every force, there is an equal and opposite force.	f. friction
____	7. force produced by round objects between surfaces	g. Newton's third law of motion
____	8. two forces that are opposite and unequal	h. fluid friction
____	9. An object acted on by unbalanced forces accelerates.	i. rolling friction
____	10. force produced when two objects slide over one another	j. balanced forces

Name _____ Date _____

Work and Machines

SECTION D WORKBOOK

Science Concept
Machines change the effect of applied forces.

Vocabulary (pages F94–F96)

| work | power | machine |

Lesson 1 Summary (pages F71–F73)

As you read the summary, fill in the blanks with vocabulary terms from above. Then complete the problems that follow.

_____ is the use of a force to make something move in the same direction as the force. To find out how much work you have done, you can use the equation *Work equals force times distance.* In this equation, force is measured in newtons. Distance is measured in meters. A unit of work is 1 newton-meter, which is equal to 1 joule. A *joule* is the unit of measure of work.

_____ is the amount of work done in a certain period of time. To find power, use the equation *Power equals work divided by time.* Work is given in joules. Time is measured in seconds. So, power is the number of joules per second.

1. Carlos attached a bag of pebbles to a spring scale. The scale registered 50 newtons. Then Carlos lifted the bag of pebbles to a height of 2 meters. How much work did Carlos do? Show your work. **(page F71)**

2. Kim lifted the same bag of pebbles that Carlos used. She lifted the bag to a height of 2 meters in 2 seconds. How much power did Kim use? Show your work. **(page F73)**

Name _____ Date _____

Lesson 2 Summary (pages F74–F76)

As you read the summary, fill in the blank with a vocabulary term from page F16. Then complete the concept map and answer the question that follows.

A _____ is any device that makes a task easier to do. The use of machines involves two types of work: *work input* and *work output*. Work input is the effort you supply. Work output is the work done by the machine. A machine does not increase the amount of work done. Machines make the task easier by changing the size or direction of the force needed to do the work or by decreasing the amount of force you need to use.

The work output of a machine is never greater than the work input. Sometimes the work output is less than the work input. Some of the work the machine must do is to overcome the force of friction.

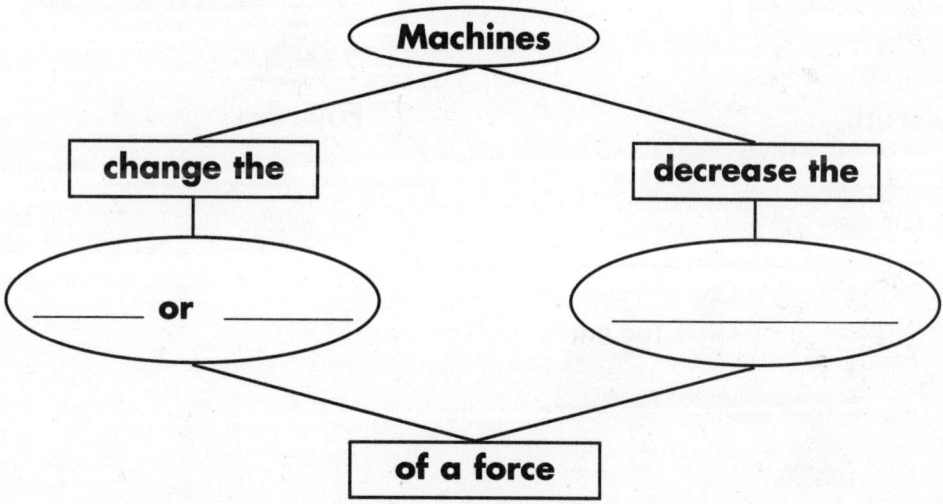

Why is a machine never 100 percent efficient? (page F76)

_____
_____
_____
_____
_____

Name_____ Date_____

Lesson 3 Summary (pages F77–F89)

Read the summary, and then answer the questions that follow.

Machines may be simple or compound. A *simple machine* has only one or two parts. A *compound machine* is made up of two or more simple machines. Some common simple machines are the lever, the inclined plane (or ramp), the screw, the wedge, the wheel and axle, and the pulley.

1. Label the effort and resistance in each diagram. Then identify the class of lever. **(page F79)**

a. _____

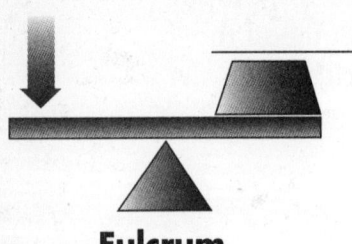

_____-class lever

b. _____

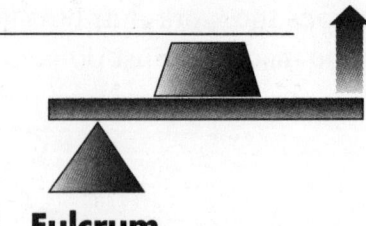

_____-class lever

c. _____

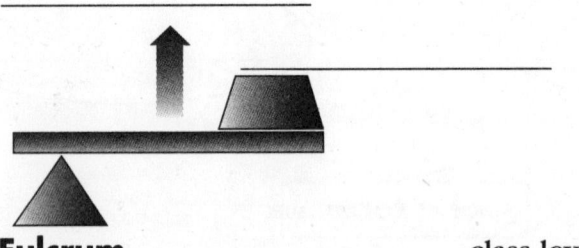

_____-class lever

2. Name six simple machines. **(pages F77–F87)**

_____

_____

3. What is the difference between a simple machine and a compound machine? **(pages F77, F88–F89)**

_____

_____

_____

Name _____ Date _____

Review the Main Ideas

- Work is the use of a force to make something move in the same direction as the force.
- A unit of work is a newton-meter, which is equal to a joule.
- Power is the amount of work done in a certain period of time.
- Power is the number of joules per second.
- A machine is any device that makes a task easier to do.
- Machines can change the size or direction of the force needed to do the work or decrease the amount of force you need to use.
- The work output of a machine is never greater than the input.
- Machines may be either simple or compound.
- A simple machine has only one or two parts; a compound machine is made up of two or more simple machines.

Check the Facts

Underline the best answer.

1. Power is defined as ...   **a.** force times distance.   **b.** energy in a machine.   **c.** work done in a certain period of time.

2. A joule is ...   **a.** a valuable gem.   **b.** a measure of the amount of work.   **c.** a measure of the strength of a machine.

3. A machine can ...   **a.** change the size of a force.   **b.** change the direction of a force.   **c.** decrease the amount of force.   **d.** do all the things mentioned in a, b, and c.

4. The comparison of a machine's work output to the work input is ...
   a. power.   **b.** efficiency.   **c.** resistance.   **d.** work.

5. Which is not a simple machine?   **a.** a crowbar   **b.** a roller coaster   **c.** a steering wheel   **d.** a seesaw

6. Using a force to make something move in the direction of the force is ...   **a.** power.   **b.** friction.   **c.** efficiency.   **d.** work.

7. Suppose you lifted a book that weighs 24 newtons. You lifted the book 2 meters off the ground. How much work would you have done?   **a.** 12 joules   **b.** 48 joules   **c.** 24 joules   **d.** 240 joules

8. Which is not an example of a lever?   **a.** a wheelbarrow   **b.** a crowbar   **c.** a nutcracker   **d.** a ramp

Section D • Work and Machines